Golden Legends

*Images of Abyssinia,
Samuel Johnson to
Bob Marley*

The History of Rasselas, Prince of Abissinia. Philadelphia, 1850.

GOLDEN LEGENDS

Images of Abyssinia,
Samuel Johnson to Bob Marley

❖

W. B. CARNOCHAN

STANFORD GENERAL BOOKS

An Imprint of Stanford University Press

Stanford, California 2008

Stanford University Press
Stanford, California

Printed in the United States of America on acid-free, archival-quality paper

Library of Congress Cataloging-in-Publication Data
Carnochan, W. B.
   Golden legends : images of Abyssinia, Samuel Johnson to Bob Marley /
W. B. Carnochan.
      p.   cm.
   Includes bibliographical references and index.
   ISBN 978-0-8047-6098-0 (casebound : alk. paper)
   1. Ethiopia—In literature. 2. Travelers' writings, English—History and
criticism. 3. English literature—History and criticism. I. Title.
   PR149.E84C37   2008
   820.9—dc22   2008019330

Designed by Susan Wilson.

To the memory of Jack Bate, teacher and friend, in whose class I first discovered the Happy Valley many years ago.

ACKNOWLEDGMENTS

Many thanks to: everyone in the Stanford University Libraries for taking so much interest in the interests of others; Mark Tewfik at Maggs Brothers, London, for bibliographic and other help; Norris Pope at the Stanford University Press for good advice; Susan Wilson for the elegance of her design; Ben Zlotkin for a handsome printing of an earlier version of the book; Susan Sebbard for her very careful eye; Matthew Garrett for careful attention to detail in compiling the notes and bibliography; Terry Castle for a roster of some who have "gone native"; Arnold Rampersad for making sure I didn't go astray in the territory of the Rastas; Wosene Worke Kosrof and Patricia DiRubbo for insights into contemporary Ethiopia; Alexander Maitland, Wilfred Thesiger's biographer, for sharing personal memories of Thesiger, and those other biographers whose work I have drawn on regularly; Abraham Verghese whose forthcoming novel, set in Ethiopia, promises to write a new chapter in the story; Ann Schlee for invaluable information and unflagging interest; and Brigitte, for the last thirty years.

Contents

I
N MAY 1981, BOB MARLEY DIED AT THE AGE OF THIRTY-SIX. Anyone
who had heard his music was shaken. Anyone who had seen him
perform—but was unaware of the ravenous cancer that killed him—
was astonished. The energy and convulsive grace that marked his
stage appearances seemed as if they could go on forever. There was
fury in the music. The Rastafarian world was a whirling current that
swept thought away. I saw Marley perform at a concert in San Diego
on a summer night, a breeze coming off the sea. He sang the songs
everyone knew, "No Woman, No Cry," "I Shot the Sheriff." But it
was the perpetual movement that was unforgettable. A year or two
later, he was dead.

Not long before he died, while being treated for cancer, Marley
was baptized into the Ethiopian Orthodox Church, taking the name
Berhane Selassie, "light of the Trinity." All of Jamaica mourned his
death. The funeral was celebrated by "his eminence Abouna
Yesehaq," who had also officiated at the baptism, "Archbishop of the
Ethiopian Orthodox Church in the Western Hemisphere, assisted
by Priests and Deacons of the Ethiopian Orthodox Church in
Jamaica." The service was conducted in Ge'ez—the ancient liturgical language of Ethiopia, in Amharic, and in English. A thousand
years of Western enchantment with the idea of Ethiopia had reached
an unpredictable yet climactic moment.[1]

CHAPTER ONE

The Call of Abyssinia: Father Lobo, Samuel Johnson, and Rasselas

IN 1603 THE PORTUGUESE JESUIT PEDRO PÁEZ arrived in the country now called Ethiopia from Yemen, bringing with him a knowledge of the local languages, acquired in Yemen, that served his mission well. He converted the emperor to Roman Catholicism (thus inciting a bloody civil war that ended with the emperor's abdication). In 1620 he published a history of Ethiopia, but it was never translated into English, and British knowledge of this far-away land can best be dated to 1682, when an Ethiopian history by the German Lutheran scholar Job (or Hiob) Ludolf, a polymath and friend of Leibniz, was translated from the Latin by John Phillips, John Milton's nephew and sometime ward, as *A New History of Ethiopia. Being a Full and Accurate Description of the Kingdom of Abessinia, Vulgarly, Though Erroneously Called the Empire of Prester John.* The vulgar error would especially have caught the eye of readers: Prester John, supposedly a Christian emperor of immense wealth, power and dominion, had been for hundreds of years a towering figure in the European imagination, possessor of vast territories on the cartographers' maps, ruler of lands where, perhaps, could be found the earthly paradise. At first, his domain was thought to be India; later, Abyssinia. But whatever the real story, assuming the legend had any substance in fact, the lands of Prester John were saturated in fantasies of a strange and gaudy Utopia. When Ludolf, accomplished in many languages (he had learned Amharic from an Ethiopian monk in Rome), turned to the legend of Prester John, he was invoking a figure who had haunted the European mind. Even though he regards the story of Prester John as a Portuguese fable and dismisses it in his text with a casual shrug, his title would have drawn readers in.[1]

A half-century later, in 1735, there appeared the fiction that, in its eventual sequel, ensured Ethiopia's permanent and prominent place in the British imagination. This was Samuel Johnson's abridgement of the *Voyage to Abyssinia* by the Portuguese Jesuit, Father Jerónimo Lobo. It was Johnson's first book. The translation of a translation by the French scholar Joachim Le Grand, it did not sell particularly well, but it was the precursor to a great fiction that followed another twenty-five years later, first published as *The Prince of Abissinia; a Tale* (1759) and long familiar as *The History of Rasselas, Prince of Abyssinia* or, simply, *Rasselas*.[2] Without *Rasselas,* the canon of English fiction would be much poorer and the imprint of Ethiopia on the British mind perhaps considerably less. When I first read *Rasselas* more than fifty years ago, I sensed even then that Johnson's Ethiopia was somehow different—different, that is, from other imaginary lands like Montesquieu's Persia or Oliver Goldsmith's China. Years later, flying from Axum to Addis Ababa, I looked out at the stark landscape below and thought that a small patch of green, just visible among the mountains, must be the Happy Valley. The seeds of this book seem to have been sown in the cloistered, quite happy valley of Cambridge, Massachusetts, in the early 1950s.

What could have induced the young Samuel Johnson, a poor lad from the midlands then in his mid-twenties, to translate so unlikely a work, as it might seem to us, as a Portuguese Jesuit's account of his travels? One reason was money: Johnson's Birmingham publisher paid him five guineas, several hundred dollars in today's currency. And the literature of travel, to anywhere and everywhere by almost anybody, was hugely popular. Only nine years before, Swift had published *Gulliver's Travels,* of which Johnson was later to say, famously and (I think) not a little enviously: "When once you have thought of big men and little men, it is very easy to do all the rest." Though *Gulliver* made splendid fun of travellers who came home (if indeed they had ever left) and spun preposterous tales, it did not abate the travel craze. What it did do was to make travel writers more careful with their facts and their audience more on the lookout for fabrications. It is not surprising that the young Johnson, careful of his reputation, praises the unsensational character of Lobo's Abyssinian narrative; or that he told Boswell he had undertaken it because he thought it might be "useful and profitable" —profitable, that is, to the general reader.[3]

Lobo "has amused his reader with no romantick absurdities or incredible fictions," Johnson wrote; "whatever he relates, whether true or not, is at least probable." His narrative is "modest and unaffected." He has "copied nature from the life." He does not populate his tale with "basilisks that destroy with their eyes" nor with crocodiles that "devour their prey [with] tears" nor with cataracts that (literally) deafen those who live nearby. Here are "no regions cursed with irremediable barrenness, or bless'd with spontaneous fecundity, no perpetual gloom or unceasing sunshine." And here is neither Utopia nor anti-Utopia, "no Hottentots without religion, polity, or articulate language, no Chinese perfectly polite."[4] We could be looking forward to Lonely Planet's guide to Ethiopia. But did Johnson's readers really want narrative sobriety? And did he really believe that he was attracted to Lobo's account because it avoided romantic absurdities? Johnson would spend a lifetime exposing the human passion for illusion, but he was good at displaying its snares because he was thoroughly, first-handedly, aware of its power. His praise of Lobo for avoiding absurd fictions did not help sales. Maybe it even turned off potential buyers. Nor was the praise wholly true, in its bare-bones version of Lobo's narrative, to the text that Johnson placed before the public. Ethiopia is a kingdom of the imagination where dream and reality intertwine, and Johnson was not immune to dreaming. Much later in his life, when he fulfilled a long-standing dream of travelling to the Hebrides, he found in the Highlands mountains and cataracts that brought back to him the image of Ethiopia.[5]

If Lobo's narrative has no basilisks that kill with a glance, it does have a snake whose breath kills at a distance: "[A]s I lay on the ground, I perceiv'd myself seiz'd with a pain which forc'd me to rise, and saw about four yards from me one of those serpents that dart their poison at a distance. Although I rose before he came very near me, I yet felt the effects of his poisonous breath, and, if I had lain a little longer, had certainly died." There are so many snakes, "continually creeping between our legs," in one area that it is "scarcely passable." We catch a glimpse, though only a glimpse, of a unicorn: "In the province of Agaus, has been seen the unicorn, that beast so much talk'd of, and so little known; the prodigious swiftness with which this creature runs from one wood into another, has given me no opportunity of examining it particularly, yet I have had so near a sight of it as to be able to give some description."[6] We learn that the Abyssinians' "most elegant treat is raw beef newly kill'd," a custom that no longer strikes us as improbable but one that, when later vividly described by the Scottish traveller James Bruce, earned him disbelief and abuse. And the landscape touches the extremes of desert—"parching thirst, burning sands, and a sultry climate"—and heavenly oases, "the pleasures of shady trees, the refreshment of a clear stream, and the luxury of a cooling breeze."[7]

Finally, Lobo comes to the great and mysterious Nile, beginning in a bottomless spring, then coursing through Lake Tana with "so violent a rapidity" that it "may be distinguish'd through all the passage," then issuing from the lake in a cataract, "one of the most beautiful waterfalls in the world," that "rushes precipitately from the top of a high rock" and "may be heard to a considerable distance"— though without deafening the "neighbouring inhabitants." Deafening or not, the grandeur of Tissisat Falls stirs even the neutral observer: "here begins the greatness of the Nile." The river is epic in length; in the catalogue of its tributaries: "the Gemma, the Keltu, the Branso and other less rivers;" and in the roll-call of kingdoms and provinces that it passes through: Begemder, Amhara, Olaca, Choaa, Damote, Goiama, Bezamo, Damot, Gamarcausa, Fazulo, Ombarca. The roll-call of names, ever since Homer, signifies grandeur. As these strange Abyssinian names flow past, the reader submits to a sense of wonder without worrying about the geography.[8]

In the years between his translation of Lobo and *Rasselas*, Johnson became the literary colossus of his day, above all as the author of the *Dictionary* (1755), that massive and perhaps unparalleled effort of intellection, imagination and perseverance. From 1750 to 1752 he had also pleased the public with his periodical *The Rambler*, a somewhat somber marriage of sage moralizing and dramatic incident—including, in two late episodes, "The History of Ten Days of Seged, Emperour of Ethiopia." The oriental tale was becoming à la mode, and Johnson catered to the fashion. Not that every "oriental tale" had to do with the orient: two other late *Ramblers* tell the lovers' story of "Anningait and Ajut, a Greenland History." Other of Johnson's tales are set in India and Samarkand. None takes much account of place. The "orient" of these tales is usually a vague location of the mind, no matter where it happens to be set. That is true as well of the story of Seged, "lord of Ethiopia"—a typical Johnsonian fable, like *Rasselas,* of elusive happiness. Seeking a respite from his labors as "monarch of forty nations," Seged orders a palace to be built on an island in a lake, recalling Lake Tana, "an island cultivated only for pleasure" in a paradise of groves and arbors and bubbling fountains: "All that could solace the sense, or flatter the fancy, all that industry could extort from nature, or wealth furnish to art, all that conquest could seize, or beneficence attract, was collected together, and every perception of delight was excited and gratified." Of course it all comes to naught. A crocodile, rising from the lake, terrifies the princesses. Jealousy infects the court. Sad memories invade Seged's repose. One of his daughters dies. And with that, "[h]ere was an end of jollity."[9]

Seven years later, needing money for his mother's funeral, Johnson thought of Ethiopia once again and, in a week's time (Sir Joshua Reynolds told Boswell), he wrote *Rasselas.* If it took him only a week, he had stored a great deal of Ethiopian lore in his head. And this time Ethiopia became, as Abyssinia, not just an oriental convenience but a place he imagined in his mind's eye. Seged might be the ruler of almost anywhere. Rasselas is, memorably, prince of an Abyssinia that emerges from Johnson's familiarity with Lobo, Ludolf, and others who helped bring the kingdom into European consciousness. With its Happy Valley, Johnson's Abyssinia feeds the longings for an earthly paradise. With its high mountains, harsh spaces, and rocky prisons, it provides a contrasting template of imagery matching the late eighteenth-century infatuation with the Gothic and the sublime. Though he never saw the mountains of

Ethiopia, Ludolf describes them with awe: "Here are many *Aorni,* or Rocks of an incredible height and ruggedness, in so much, that … they strike a terror into the Beholders; the *Alps* and *Pyreneans,* compar'd with the *Abessine* Mountains, are but low Hills." In fact the highest of the Alps is higher than the highest of Ethiopian mountains, but Ludolf succumbs to the rapture and terror of the heights, and the equivalent rapture of royal captivities. Often he relies on a narrative history by the Portuguese Jesuit Balthasar Telles. The mountain where the royal sons are locked up, according to "Tellezius," is *"almost impregnable, every way steep, prodigiously high, and in the form of a Castle made all of Free-Stone."* And: "between these Mountains are immense Gulphs, and dreadful Profundities; which because the Sight cannot fathom, Fancy takes them for Abysses; whose bottoms *Tellezius* will have to be the Center of the Earth." Impregnable mountain prisons, immense gulphs, dreadful profundities that reach the center of the earth—these are the raw materials of terror; and, in Edmund Burke's account, "terror is in all cases whatsoever … the ruling principle of the sublime."[10]

Burke had published his "philosophical enquiry" on the sublime and beautiful—"true criticism, "Johnson called it—in 1757, two years before *Rasselas.* The first edition of Piranesi's fantastic prisons, the *Carceri* (1745), preceded *Rasselas* by fourteen years. Horace Walpole's *The Castle of Otranto,* usually called the first Gothic novel, followed in 1765. And as early as 1688, the critic John Dennis, later Pope's whipping boy as "Sir Tremendous Longinus," had experienced "delightful Horrour" and "terrible joy" as he crossed the Alps. *Rasselas* came into a world that cultivated an ever-growing passion for all things mountainous or sublime. With Abyssinia as his setting, Johnson would have excited expectations; and in the event, his imaginary landscape conforms to the gathering taste for sublimity while invoking as well the terrestrial paradise, forever lush and green.[11]

In the Happy Valley, reminiscent of Seged's happy island, all the animals of the earth frisk and play or, like the "solemn elephant," repose in the shade. A lake and a great cataract recall Lobo and the beginnings of the Nile: "From the mountains on every side, rivulets descended that filled all the valley with verdure and fertility, and formed a lake in the middle inhabited by fish of every species, and frequented by every fowl whom nature has taught to dip the wing in water." But the mountains are all around, their caverns measureless to man: "This lake discharged its superfluities by a stream which entered a dark cleft of the mountain on the northern side, and fell with dreadful noise from precipice to precipice till it was heard no more." The noise may not deafen but is "dreadful," inspiring dread. And the Happy Valley, though a chamber of delights, is sealed from the world outside. The only way in or out leads through a cavern with "gates of iron" at the entrance, "forged by the artificers of ancient days, so massy that no man could, without the help of engines, open or shut them." Johnson knew nothing (we can assume) of the *Carceri,* but the massive gates and engines at the entrance to the Happy Valley bring Piranesi's fantasies exactly to mind.[12]

Eventually Rasselas and the philosopher-poet Imlac—his name seems to have been inspired by a fourteenth-century prince in Ludolf's account—find a way to escape the Happy Valley and, having dug their way out, emerge on "the top of a mountain" where they "beheld the Nile, yet a narrow current, wandering beneath them." "Prospect" poems surveying the landscape from a height were another popular poetic exercise of the time, a tradition of long views that became a common marker of the sublime. Burke wrote: "Extension is either in length, height, or depth. Of these the length strikes the least; an hundred yards of even ground will never work such an effect as a tower an hundred yards high, or a rock or mountain of that altitude. I am apt to imagine likewise, that height is less grand than depth; and that we are more struck at looking down from a precipice, than at looking up at an object of equal height." The long view of the great Nile while it is still a narrow current, and from a high precipice, touches the most tender nerve of sublimity.[13]

At the same time, Johnson worries that the acrophobic sublimity of heights and depths springs from emotions that are insufficiently "manly;" the sublime Abyssinia of his imagination is an ambiguous site of feeling. He assigns the most acute sensations of vertigo not to Rasselas and Imlac but to the women who have joined the men, Rasselas's favorite sister and her maidservant. As they begin their descent, "the princess and her maid turned their eyes towards every part, and, seeing nothing to bound their prospect, considered themselves as in danger of being lost in a dreary vacuity. They stopped and trembled." They see "nothing" and nothingness. They fear the vacuity of the abyss that reaches to the center of things. "'I am almost afraid,' said the princess, 'to begin a journey of which I cannot perceive an end'." Unlike the princess and her maid, however, the prince and the philosopher resist as best they can the rapture of the heights—Rasselas because he thinks it unworthy of him, Imlac because he is a philosopher. Rasselas "felt nearly the same emotions, though he thought it more manly to conceal them." Imlac merely "smiled at their terrours." A constant tension is at play between Abyssinia, with its grandeur, and the lowland world of ordinary life.[14]

From this point on, the setting of the story is not Abyssinia but Egypt, and—except for the travellers' fateful excursion to the pyramids—Egypt has only modest importance as a setting: no high mountains, no happy valleys, here. Cairo is to Abyssinia as the plain to the mountains, a level field of ordinary life with its hopes of happiness and inevitable disappointments. The travellers' first impression of Cairo could be any visitor's first impression of London: "They now entered the town, stunned by the noise, and offended by the crowds," just as Johnson was stunned when he first arrived in London after his boyhood in the provincial town of Lichfield: "The attention of a new-comer is generally first struck by the multiplicity of cries that stun him in the streets." The opulence of Cairo matches that of London, and the remoteness of the Happy Valley matches that of Lichfield, though that is hardly how Johnson thought of his boyhood home. Still, the parallel is telling: "Happiness is enjoyed," Johnson wrote, "only in proportion as it is known; and such is the state or folly of man, that it is known only by experience of its contrary: we who have long lived amidst the conveniences of a town immensely populous, have scarce an idea of a place where desire cannot be gratified by money. In order to have a just sense of this artificial plenty, it is necessary to have passed some time in a distant colony, or those parts of our island which are thinly inhabited." The "artificial" plenty and conveniences of London or Cairo are set against the idea of a place, Lichfield or the Happy Valley, where desire, for better or for worse, "cannot be gratified by money." Lichfield, Stourbridge, and Edial were the small Midland places, far from the heart of things, where Johnson spent his life before coming to London at the age of twenty-seven. And, however much he loved London, he knew that without Lichfeld, London could not have been what it was. Without Cairo, Abyssinia also could not have been what it was.[15]

Probably I am not alone in finding Egypt a letdown after the mountain fastness of the Happy Valley: a grey blanket of feeling hangs over Cairo in contrast to the clear air of the Abyssinian mountains. Though the happiness of the Happy Valley may be a passing illusion for its inhabitants, what the reader takes away is not the tedium of paradise so much as the carceral grandeur of the place and the fantastic leap of the imagination that it takes to get there. If Johnson relies for solace on the everyday life of the lowlands, he also recognizes intensely the profusion of false hopes and idle dreams that the travellers find in Egypt. After their escape, they make their way gradually to Cairo where, on first arrival, they "find every man happy," only to discover how shaky is every scheme of felicity. Pastoral fantasies, rakish excess, Stoic indifference, it does not matter: happiness is an *ignis fatuus* of the mind. Among the sites of imaginary felicity that might have been included in Johnson's catalogue is Abyssinia itself, both sublime and paradisiacal.[16]

In the famous, and famously opaque, last chapter of *Rasselas* ("in which nothing is concluded"), the travellers, confined to their house by the annual inundation of the Nile, discuss what they have seen and learned and what they can hope for. The princess proposes to found "a college of learned women." Her servant wants to become a prioress at a convent. Rasselas longs for "a little kingdom" of his own where he can "administer justice in his own person," but such are human yearnings that he is always expanding his imaginary dominion and "adding to the number of his subjects." Imlac is willing to drift along the stream of life. Of these wishes, they decide, "none could be obtained." The desire to drift along the stream of life does not seem beyond reach, but Johnson's conclusion reminds us that a printer's boy was probably knocking on the door as he wrote, awaiting the final pages of the manuscript: Johnson told Sir Joshua Reynolds that he sent *Rasselas* "to the press in portions as it was written." The story had to be ended somehow, and the last sentence takes the travellers back to their beginning: "They deliberated a while what was to be done, and resolved, when the inundation should cease, to return to Abissinia."[17]

Where do the travellers actually return? Is it (could it be?) to the Happy Valley? Several decades ago, these questions were intently debated.[18] But the debate was waged on assumptions out of touch with reality: that writers—or great writers, anyway—always know what they are doing; that close reading will ferret out their meanings, even when meanings outstrip intentions; and that, because Johnson is a great writer, *Rasselas* must be a coherent fiction. In this critical calculus, no attention goes to the conditions of pressure and haste under which *Rasselas* was written; to the larger truth that even Homer nods; nor, above all, to the double feelings evoked by the fantastical (but inhuman) perfection of the Happy Valley, on the one hand, and the ordinary (but human) imperfection of Cairo, on the other. In the first chapter we learn that "those, on whom the iron gate had once closed, were never suffered to return"—and that might seem to settle the issue. But perhaps (reading closer) it is only visiting performers who, after one visit, are barred from return. Yet (surely) Rasselas would be treated on his return as a fugitive and, as a prince of the blood, a threat to imperial order. It is better to set this guesswork aside. The travellers return because they have been a long time away, and the ambiguous Eden of Abyssinia is home. It is the Odyssean story in a more somber, more uncertain vein. A sense of homecoming is palpable though Penelope is not waiting.[19]

The exotic setting of the Happy Valley both suits its time and looks ahead. The carceral representations of sublimity, reminiscent of Piranesi, anticipate the fantastical, dizzying spaces of an oriental extravaganza like William Beckford's *Vathek* (1786). The image of the earthly paradise looks ahead to Coleridge's "Kubla Khan" (1798) and its sacred river, its pleasure dome, and the Abyssinian maid playing her dulcimer. Cairo is the anti-Abyssinia. And, in its representations over the centuries, Abyssinia is an antidote to the workaday. Between the ordinary world of Cairo and the extraordinary world of Abyssinia, the pendulum of feeling swings.

It was Johnson, a diligent champion of the everyday, who opened the floodgates. He would have been surprised to learn how deeply Abyssinian dreams and the Happy Valley have imprinted themselves on the Western mind. A San Francisco map from the 1850s shows a Happy Valley, and an adjacent Pleasant Valley, just south of the main thoroughfare of Market Street. Look in an atlas and you can find a Happy Valley in Labrador and another in New Mexico. Look on the Web, and you find a "Happy Valley Laundry"; "Happy Valley Orthodontics"; "Happy Valley Pet Grooming"; and "Happy Valley Country Club." There is a "Happy Valley Race-course" in Hong Kong. It is a fair guess that proprietors of these enterprises are often unaware of their great original—and therefore don't know that it all began in Abyssinia.

CHAPTER TWO

"Going Native": James Bruce, Mansfield Parkyns, Richard Burton

I N DAVID LEAN S FILM, LAWRENCE OF ARABIA (1962), there comes a
moment when a British officer wonders if Lawrence has "gone
native"—not, in the eyes of colonial officials or regimental officers,
a good thing to do. Nor, eventually, did Lawrence himself underes-
timate the dangers—different in kind from any that would have
troubled his superiors: "[T]he efforts for these years to live in the
dress of the Arabs, and to imitate their mental foundation, quitted
me of my English self, and let me look at the West and its conventions with new eyes: they destroyed it all for me. At the same time I
could not sincerely take on the Arab skin: it was an affectation only."
The Lawrence romance has entranced very many, sometimes to the
neglect of its ambiguities: "Easily was a man made an infidel, but
hardly might he be converted to another faith. I had dropped one
form and not taken on the other, and was become like Mohammed's
coffin in our legend, with a resultant feeling of intense loneliness in
life, and a contempt, not for other men, but for all they do." His
double life, Lawrence feared, had cost him the better part of his san-
ity: "[M]adness was very near, as I believe it would be near the man
who could see things through the veils at once of two customs, two
educations, two environments." His understanding of what it meant

to go native involves difficult matters of identity and belief.[1]

In an "imperial archive," maintained on the Web by students at the Queen's University in Belfast and "dedicated to the study of Literature, Imperialism, Postcolonialism," "going native" is, predictably, a "key concept." Participation "in native rituals" and adoption of "local customs regarding food, dress, and entertainment" are part of the story, but sex, especially in black Africa, is the main thing. The students at Queen's University get that right. Thus: "The phobia that even mere cohabitation with the natives, or exposure to the harsh humidity of the foreign climate could result in moral and physical degeneration was widespread." And: "Copulation with a native woman was considered a serious menace to the wholesomeness of the white race by the debauched blacks." Copulation by a white woman with a native man would be still worse. But how much all this leaves out. What the imperial attitude fails to notice is that going native, if we do not limit the meaning of "native," is something that happens all the time; and that, as Lawrence knew, the character, both inward and outward, of the experience outstrips anything that a post-colonial description, accurate so far as it goes, can convey. Mohammed's coffin, in the legend that Lawrence remembers, was suspended somewhere halfway between earth and heaven.[2]

A whole spectrum of behavior could count as "going native" if the idea were not so loaded with colonial connotations and so lacking in nuance that, once scrutinized, it is better set aside. The spectrum runs from dressing up in the spirit of carnival, at one end, to complete immersion in the dress, food, language, customs, and sexual practices of a different culture, at the other. Imagine, difficult though it may be, a twenty-five year old Frenchman who comes to the United States, manages to lose most of his French accent, marries an American woman in Las Vegas, and becomes a baseball fan.

Then remember all the other cases of cross-cultural migration, and structural differences quickly fade (as opposed to other differences, including the psychological) between the experience of, say, Gauguin in Tahiti and our imaginary Frenchman who loves baseball. Even so, certain markers are telling. Will our Frenchman ever go back to France? Will our Englishman, or Englishwoman, go back to England? And for what reasons? Maybe Penelope awaits at home after the seductions of Circe, Calypso, and the Sirens. Maybe a higher destiny summons. Moses leaves an Ethiopian wife to lead the Jews out of Egypt. Aeneas dallies with Dido, then sets off to found Rome. Parsifal's father Gahmuret takes a Moorish Queen as his wife, leaves her pregnant, then fathers the Lord-to-be of the Grail. Whether the motive is a summons of destiny or a longing for home, the romance of "going native," like that of any traveller's journey, often amounts to an interlude in space and time.

Britishers like Lawrence typically head home to the serenity of their own countryside. After his strange, tormented, and dangerous life, Lawrence retired to a cottage called Clouds Hill in Dorset—although, remote and tiny as it was, it signified his loneliness, not the usual alliance between those who return and the local gentry. And the back roads of Dorset, in a twist of fate, turned out to be more dangerous than anything that had gone before; soon after settling at Clouds Hill, Lawrence was killed in an accident on his beloved motorcycle. His fate was in keeping with the intensities of the life he had led and the agitations of his heart. Many another traveller died comfortably at home in bed.

In the line of those who went at least part way native, two eighteenth-century voyagers, not to Abyssinia but to Turkey, were forerunners. These were Lady Mary Wortley Montagu and her scapegrace son Edward. Both of them were flamboyant, Edward especially so. They were also, in their separate ways, brave. On the spectrum of identification with another culture they were closer to the comedy of dressing up than to serious immersion, but their passion for inhabiting worlds other than their own anticipated much of what, in other times and places, was to come. They made a large contribution to the British institution, as it became, of cross-cultural adventuring.

In March 1717, Lady Mary, newly arrived with her husband in Adrianople, the Thracian seat of the Turkish emperor, went shopping for her spring wardrobe. On the first of April, she wrote her sister, the Countess of Mar, to describe her new outfit. It included "a pair of drawers," made of rose-colored damask, with a brocade of silver flowers, reaching modestly all the way to her new white kid shoes, themselves embroidered with gold. Her smock, of "fine white silk Gause," was embroidered and closed at the neck with a diamond button—but it left "the shape and colour of the bosom very well to be distinguished through it." Then we learn, now in the third person, the many sumptuous details of Turkish dress, without always knowing how far Lady Mary may have gone in emulation. Turkish hair adornments are especially grand: on one side of the head, an embroidered cap; on the other, "the ladies are at liberty to shew their fancies"—sometimes flowers, sometimes a plume of feathers, but "the most general fashion is a large Bouquet of Jewels, made like natural flowers, that is, the buds of Pearl, the roses, of different colour'd Rubys, the Jess'mines of Di'monds, Jonquils of Topazes, etc., so well set and enammell'd, tis hard to imagine any thing of that kind so beautifull." Portraits of Lady Mary in her Turkish habit show her well-embroidered and bejeweled, with a floral brooch on her head-dress—a large bouquet, it seems, of jewels. Probably she went all the way Turkish in the luxuries of dress, no matter how diffidently she switches from the first to the third person in reporting to her sister.

Perhaps she worried that the Countess (or her Jacobite husband) would be wary of oriental excess. She loved oriental excess herself, taking a giddy delight in the description of her new habit and the freedom that (paradoxically) it conferred, but perhaps she also wanted to distance herself, just a little, from a transfiguration that left her suspended between two worlds.[3]

Lady Mary's costume, however splendid, was also a matter of tact and convenience: when in Rome, do as the Romans do. Turkish women thought that European necklines were risqué, and Lady Mary wanted no scandal, though she reassures her sister that "the shape and colour" of her bosom remain on display. She also stopped short of joining naked Turkish women in their communal bath, somewhat to the damage of her recent reputation: should she not have joined in the fun? Adapting to local custom, at least in the right spirit, is more likely these days to garner praise.[4] But if Lady Mary was circumspect, her scapegrace son was not: even in the long line of English eccentrics, Edward Wortley Montagu stands out. And, late in his life, he adopted, at least in dress and manner, a style as Turkish as that of the Turks themselves.[5]

Returning with his parents from Constantinople, Edward was shipped off, at the age of five, to Westminster School—where he absorbed more than the usual number of lashes from a sadistic schoolmaster and twice ran away. At thirteen he went up briefly to Oxford, studied oriental languages, and made his compliant young landlady the first of his many conquests. With a mixture of exasperation and perhaps a covert appreciation for the boy's precocity, Lady Mary told her sister that "[m]y young rogue of a son is the most ungovernable little rake that ever played truant." The rest of Edward's life was a picaresque saga of marriages, gambling debts, imprisonment, and an extreme taste for the exotic. Famously, he paraded around London for a time wearing different satin suits with diamond buttons for each day of the week, diamond shoe-buckles, and an iron wig so realistic that, Horace Walpole said, "you literally would not know it from hair." The wig, Walpole believed, got him elected to the Royal Society. And through all this picaresque career ran a conspicuous and continuous thread: the lure of the orient. After his brief spell at Oxford and after his first marriage ended, he enrolled at Leyden to study with the foremost scholar of Arabic (and also Hebrew) in Europe, the Dutch philologist Albert Schultens. Twenty years later, intending a grand tour of eastern lands, he enrolled at Leyden once again to brush up. "Languages," as his biographer adroitly puts it, "were a more serious matter to Edward than marriages."[6]

In 1767, fifty years after he had first arrived in Constantinople as a young child, Edward Wortley Montagu returned as a traveller, this time with all the appurtenances of a Turk. He had a beard and a turban, he spoke the language fluently, and he almost succeeded in having an audience with the Sultan, though it was called off at the last minute. Had he visited Mecca and Medina, as he had hoped until death intervened, he would have anticipated Richard Burton's pilgrimage of 1853 by decades. And in his final two years, he became one of the mandatory sights of Venice for young Englishmen on the Grand Tour. He put on a polished display of Turkishness for his visitors—and fostered the story that he was a by-blow of his mother's liaison with a Sultan: Lady Mary had entered the seraglio (Edward's story ran) disguised as a eunuch. With his beard and turban and scimitar, the old Turk is recognizably the descendant of the young blade who strutted about London in satin suit and diamond-buckled shoes. More extravagant than his mother, he was something of an armchair Turk in his comfortable Venetian setting—though we may think, again with Lawrence, that madness was not far off in the wings.[7]

Armchair Turk or not, slightly crazed or not, Edward Wortley Montagu had some expertise on Biblical geography, and on one occasion he faced a challenge from James Bruce, known to Boswell and others as "Abyssinian" Bruce, regarding the existence—or not—of mountains in the Sinai. Edward had travelled to the Sinai in 1764, along with the latest of his wives, and seen mountains with rock inscriptions that he had hoped, vainly, might have been the work of Moses. They were called "Gebel el Macaatab," the "Written Mountains." In a letter to Sir William Watson, an accomplished physician and experimental scientist, Edward published his findings in the Royal Society's *Transactions* for 1766. Later he was offended to learn that Bruce, then in Cairo, doubted the existence of "Gebel el Macaatab," and he wrote to Watson: "Mr. Bruce is returned from Abyssinia. He seems to doubt the existence of the Written Mountains. It is a place as well known at Cairo and amongst the Arabs, as Edinburgh is amongst us." In turn, Edward eventually had his revenge on Bruce by casting doubt on Bruce's Abyssinian narrative in a letter to the *European Magazine.* Explorers are a contentious lot. Whether Bruce had any fair reason to doubt the existence of the "Written Mountains" in the first place is uncertain. What is certain: he would not have hesitated a moment in the dispute. "Abyssinian" Bruce was never shy in expressing his opinions or acting in his own regard.[8]

❖ JAMES BRUCE

We are at the intersection of three roads. The first is the history of travel writing as associated, especially but not exclusively, with the history of empire. The second is the history of sexuality and travel as reflected not only in the history of empire but in the history of anthropology. The third is the subject of this book, different from but overlapping with the first two: representations of a single place, Abyssinia. Of these separate histories, the first has become an enormous academic industry ever since Edward Said pointed the way in *Orientalism* (1978). The second, as it has to do with the practices of anthropology, is only now coming out of the shadows. This story of the third, representations of Abyssinia, will sometimes cover the same ground as those who have brought the practices of travel writing to the fore. It will also converge with the sexual histories, as they are beginning to be known, of anthropologists and others in the field.

The first and greatest of British travellers in Abyssinia, James Bruce came from the Scottish line that went back to Robert the Bruce and Bannockburn. His mother was a Bruce, and his father David Hay took his wife's name. James was born in 1730. By the standards of the time, he grew up to be giant in stature, 6' 4" tall. He was brave, indefatigable, quarrelsome, proud, perhaps depressive and sometimes devious. He also had the gift of charm. He could have been a rival to Don Juan; his catalogue of conquests included several high-born Ethiopian women—even more, probably, than he hints at in the narrative account of his wanderings. He was a good observer of local customs. And he was the first Briton to reach the beginnings of the Blue Nile.

As with many stories of adventure and adventuring, and like that of Edward Wortley Montagu, some random chances gave Bruce's life its picaresque shape, onto which he grafted a sheer love of adventure. Before he arrived in Ethiopia, at the age of thirty-eight, he had been here, there, and everywhere. When his young first wife died only seven months after their marriage in February 1754, he set off on a fifteen-year whirlwind that took him to Portugal, Spain, France, Germany, the Netherlands, Italy, Algiers (as consul-general),

Tunis, Tripoli, Crete (on his second attempt, a shipwreck having aborted his first try), Sidon, Baalbek, Palmyra, and Egypt, where he arrived, in Arab dress, at the end of June 1768. Along the way he had acquired some medical knowledge, especially about smallpox, that served him well in Ethiopia, where the disease was rampant. Finally, in September 1769, he entered the island port of Massawa, the gateway to Ethiopia. He spent the next three years there and in the neighboring kingdom of Sennar (now part of the Sudan), all of this at a time when the countryside, suffering from convulsive tribal hostilities and warfare, was full of danger. Throughout he dressed and lived as one of the natives. He even became a local official.

Bruce's first goal was the Nile, and he reached Tissisat Falls in late spring, 1770. The sight filled him with exhilaration. Anyone who has had the good luck to see the falls will understand why: "The cataract itself was the most magnificent sight that ever I beheld." Bruce's Abyssinian sublime recalls Johnson's mountains and cataracts, and he is unwilling to share the experience, either the discovery or the sight itself, with anyone, especially not with a Portuguese Jesuit. Having to be first is the experiential sickness of explorers, and Bruce goes to great lengths to discredit his predecessor: "Jerome Lobo pretends, that he has sat under the curve, or arch, made by the projectile force of the water rushing over the precipice. He says he sat calmly at the foot of it, and looking through the curve of the stream, as it was falling, saw a number of rainbows of inconceivable beauty in this extraordinary prism." Bruce will have none of it, not least because Lobo's beautiful rainbows compete with his own image of torrential magnificence: "This however I, without hesitation, aver to be a downright falsehood." The desire to get credit for a geographical discovery and the aesthetic experience that went with it obliterates any trace of impartiality. By the time Bruce published his description of the falls in 1790, twenty years after the event, he should have known and perhaps did know, if he ever thought about it, that his visit to the falls took place during the rainy season when the flow of water was at its height, while Lobo was there during dry season. Bruce's narrative did not appear until six years after Samuel Johnson's death, and Johnson, no lover of Bruce—he had even begun to doubt that Bruce had ever been to Ethiopia—would have resented this slander of a traveller whom he admired and had presented to the English-speaking public. Bruce's parting sally again celebrates an aesthetic susceptibility, his own, at Lobo's expense: the falls "struck me with a kind of stupor, and a total oblivion of where I was, and of every other sublunary concern." He could be copying from Burke: "It was one of the most magnificent, stupendous sights in the creation, though degraded and vilified by the lies of a grovelling fanatic priest." This is curious: how Lobo's description "degrades" or "vilifies" the sight is hard to understand, except psychologically. Lobo's claim, and his rainbows also, stain the sublime purity of Bruce's vision. Lobo's account simply gets in the way, like an unwanted flaw in an otherwise perfect image.[9]

Tissisat falls did not qualify as the ultimate source of the great river, however, and it was not until November 1770, that Bruce made his way to the unremarkable stretch of springs and marshy ground that Lobo had identified as the source. Even more than the falls, the experience induces a rhetoric of rapture, not visual now for really there is little to see, but inward: "It is easier to guess than to describe the situation of my mind at that moment—standing in that spot which had baffled the genius, industry, and inquiry of both ancients and moderns, for the course of near three thousand years." It had not, of course, baffled the industrious inquiry of Father Lobo, but Bruce simply refuses to notice him: "Fame, riches and honour, had been held out for a series of ages to every individual of those myriads these princes commanded, without having produced one man capable of gratifying the curiosity of his sovereign, or wiping off this stain upon the enterprise and abilities of mankind, or adding this desideratum for the encouragement of geography. Though a mere private Briton, I triumphed, here, in my own mind, over kings and their armies." There cannot have been many more triumphal outbursts in the annals of exploration than this one by a mere private Briton, triumphing "in his mind" over kings and armies. Yet after the triumph comes something like depression. Suddenly, as Bruce finds himself thinking about the dangerous return journey that awaits him, "I found a despondency gaining ground fast upon me, and blasting the crown of laurels I had too rashly woven for myself." Surely this despondency has less to do with the journey before him, which retraces familiar if dangerous ground, than with the mind's normal experience, exaggerated here by the sheer heights of Bruce's Ethiopian high, of a hard landing upon coming back to earth. In some measure, he knew this. On the night when he arrives at the "coy fountains" of the Nile and when he is, "at that very moment, in possession of what had, for many years, been the principal object of my ambition and wishes," the demon of "indifference, which, from the usual infirmity of human nature follows, at least for a time, complete enjoyment, had taken place of it." Samuel Johnson said that we go from hope to hope, not satisfaction to satisfaction. And now Bruce finds himself longing for the quiet splendors of home. The rivers of Scotland, the Tweed, the Clyde, and the Annan, are "not inferior to the Nile in beauty." And "I began, in my sorrow, to treat the inquiry about the source of the Nile as a violent effort of a distempered fancy." Tormented, he cannot sleep: "I started from my bed in the utmost agony." Then he rushes out into the cool night and is at peace again. Like other travellers, he has been touched by something like madness.[10]

His extravagance of style and temper, combined with his hinting and winking about his amorous exploits, only added to the skepticism that greeted Bruce's return to Britain in 1774 and then, sixteen years later, the publication of his *Travels*. Yet he helped bring the skepticism on himself: not only did he cut a scandalous figure but he was very cantankerous, and his description of Ethiopian customs was more than the average Briton could well accept or imagine. Who would believe that Ethiopians sliced meat off the haunch of a living ox and consumed it raw? Or that their sexual mores so little resembled those of middle-class Britain? Or that James Bruce had actually gone to bed with, among several others, an Ethiopian princess, thus "informing queens, in naked pride"—as the satirist Peter Pindar put it, with calculated inelegance—"the feel and colour of a Scotsman's hide"?[11]

A centerpiece of Bruce's narrative is his description of Ethiopian banquets. From these banquets to Clifford Geertz's Balinese cockfight is a long road and yet, reading Bruce in the retrospective light of two centuries, one senses what is ever-present in travel narratives, the coming of the anthropological.[12] Like Lady Mary and her story of the Turkish bath, but without her openness of disclosure, Bruce confronts the anthropological problem: how to balance the roles of participant and observer? How thoroughly to take part, assuming participation is granted, in the lives and experience of others; and then, how to describe that experience and those lives in a way that both preserves and transcends the brute fact of otherness? How to diminish the distorting effects of the observing observer? Bruce's resolution is mostly to overlook the difficulties, pretending that they aren't there at all, even though he has some awareness that they are. The banquets may be a disgraceful spectacle, as Bruce concedes without really meaning it, but duty requires him to take up the unwelcome task of describing them: "I cannot avoid giving some account of this Polyphemus banquet, as far as decency will permit me; it is part of the history of a barbarous people; whatever I might wish, I cannot decline it." Of course this is window dressing. James Bruce was not one to shy away from riot and debauch.[13]

When "the spear and shield is [sic] hung up in the hall," as if the endless warfare were only a summer sport, "a number of people of the best fashion in the villages, of both sexes, courtiers in the palace, or citizens in the town, meet together to dine between twelve and one o'clock." The hour between noon and one was not the banquet hour in eighteenth-century Britain, and readers would have sensed that something surprising was coming up. These are gatherings of the *bon ton,* whether in the countryside or, where Bruce seems mainly to have observed them, in the royal city of Gondar. He was a passably good observer, and he covers everything from seating arrangements to the flaying of cattle: "All the flesh on the buttocks is cut off then, and in solid, square pieces, without bones, or much effusion of blood; and the prodigious noise the animal makes is a signal for the company to sit down to table." The bellowing of the animal is the Abyssinian equivalent of a European fanfare: let the feasting begin. And seating arrangements, at first glance, also resemble their European counterparts. "The company are so ranged that one man sits between two women," which might be the same as to say that one woman sits between two men, as in Europe. But that seems not the case here. A more careful anthropologist would not have left any uncertainty; but, however exactly it works, two women attend to the needs of one man. The man cuts a good-sized steak from the raw meat. The women cut it in small strips, then wrap it in the fermented, rubbery, pancake-like bread called injera. And, because "[n]o man in Abyssinia, of any fashion whatever, feeds himself, or touches his own meat," the women take turns stuffing the wrapped meat into his mouth. Meanwhile, Bruce lets slip as if by accident a tell-tale detail: each of the man's hands rests upon "his neighbour's knee."[14]

The men's hands on their neighbors' knees signal what comes next. The man eats his fill and drinks from "a large handsome horn." Then the women eat, and then they all drink together. Laughter and revelry fill the hall. The poor animal on which the company has feasted finally bleeds to death, and its "assassins" tear its "flesh from the bones with their teeth, like dogs." Then the climax to all this revelry: "In the mean time, those within are very much elevated; love lights all its fires, and every thing is permitted with absolute freedom. There is no coyness, no delays, no need of appointments or retirement to gratify their wishes; there are no rooms but one, in which they sacrifice both to Bacchus and to Venus." But now, with the help of the revelers themselves, Bruce draws a veil: "The two men nearest the vacuum a pair have made on the bench by leaving their seats, hold their upper garment like a screen before the two that have left." If the lovers are out of sight, however, they are not out of hearing: "if we may judge by the sound, they seem to think it as great a shame to make love in silence as to eat." The couple returns to their seats, everyone drinks their health, and in all this "not a licentious word is uttered." Lest anyone flinch from his description, Bruce adds a learned note: the behavior of the Ethiopians matches that of the ancient Cynics who made their sacrifices to Bacchus and to Venus in public view.[15]

A modern student of the human sciences would like to know more about these transactions. Who is the happy couple? Are there many happy couples? What conventions govern individual pairings? Who chooses whom? How? Are guests seated randomly or with pre-meditation? And the gallant males who hold up their garments to shield the lovers: do they get to look on or do they turn away, enhancing the veneer of modesty? Exactly how do they screen the lovers with their garments? Which garments? And so on. But the big question: what is the proto-anthropologist James Bruce doing all the while? On the track record that he posts elsewhere, and assuming some randomness among those couples who decide to couple, Bruce is more likely to have participated than only to have observed. But that is the thing he can only hint at, not reveal. Many things go on in the field that are not usually talked about.

Probably Bruce is willing, or more than willing, to let us assume he participated in the Gondar love-feasts. His biographer takes the luscious bait, no more than reasonably, and speculates that one of these parties was the occasion when Bruce consummated his relationship with Ozoro (or Waizero) Esther,[16] a formidably brutal woman, grand-daughter of the empress, and the wife—her third marriage—of the elderly and equally brutal Ras Michael, governor of Tigre province. Bruce's biographer again: "Notwithstanding her brutality, Bruce adored her." He won her devotion by successfully treating an outbreak of smallpox in the royal family that had befallen her son. In turn she protected him. And the story of their liaison has lived on in Ethiopia. I remember a guide in Gondar who pointed to the stone remnants of a building on the grounds of the seventeenth-century palace. He said it was the place where James Bruce and Esther had ... But what exactly did he say? Still, there was no mistaking the point. There was even a suggestion, if I remember right, that a child was born of the union. That story has not found its way into the record.[17]

In 1768, the very year that Bruce arrived in Massawa, Laurence Sterne published the volume that he called *A Sentimental Journey through France and Italy by Mr. Yorick*. When it comes to matters of the heart, James Bruce's *Travels to Discover the Source of the Nile* could as well have been called *A Sentimental Journey through Ethiopia and Sennar*, for his habits of disclosure are as coy as those of Mr. Yorick, who always has his hand on a chambermaid's knee. Like Yorick, Bruce kisses and tells, but never, ever too much, for sentiment, in the sense that Sterne did everything to establish, was not a crude matter of sex, nor of conquest, but of elevated feeling. Bruce, the very big Scotsman, imitates Sterne's attenuated hero and gives us not a catalogue aria but a delicate traversal of an amatory landscape. Not only, in his chronicles of the heart, was there Esther, there were Irepone, "nymph of the Nile," and Melectanea, wife of Fasil, the rebel governor of Damot who was at war with Ras Michael; and perhaps, though Bruce is very discreet, the beautiful daughter of the first minister of Sennar. For all of them Bruce expressed vast appreciation for their beauty and a tender attachment—before packing his bags and heading on his way, Aeneas-like, to whatever destiny lay ahead.[18]

Soon after he left Gondar, seeking the Nile, he received a message from Esther. She was ill—it is the trope of the suffering lover, Dido watching Aeneas depart—and urgently asked him to return "ere it would be too late," but the Nile, like Rome, calls him on: "I do believe the pursuit I was then engaged in was the only one which I would not have instantly abandoned upon such a summons. Besides the sincere attachment I had myself to her, as one of the most lovely and amiable women in the world; she was the mother of my most intimate friend." The country is on the brink of civil strife, however, that threatens Bruce's mission, and "I therefore resolved to run the risk of continuing for a time under the imputation of the foulest and basest of all sins, that of ingratitude to my benefactors." Had he died, he assures us, "I am confident … the consideration of my lying with apparent reason under that imputation would have been one of the most bitter reflections of my last moments." Of course he did not die, but the episode allows him to play his double role as an explorer acting out his destiny who is equally an eighteenth-century man of feeling, alive to the charms of the most lovely and amiable woman in the world and conscious, also, of the claims of friendship. When he returned to Gondar, the exhilaration of the Nile behind him, Esther had recovered from her illness.[19]

On his way to the Nile, Bruce had not lacked other company to console him for Esther's absence. Briefly he took up residence in the village of Geesh, near the Nile source, whose chief offered him his daughters as housekeepers. Bruce accepted "readily," not that we would have expected otherwise. The eldest of the three, aged sixteen, was "remarkably genteel, and, colour apart, her features would have made her a beauty in any country in Europe; she was, besides, very sprightly." This is Irepone, Bruce's nymph of the Nile. With her he is the perfect gentleman. He gives her presents, including an ounce of gold to defray expenses. He tells her she need not provide any accountings. And he reports: "it was impossible to be so blinded, as not to see that I had already made great progress in her affections." The perfect gentleman, the man of feeling, and the wandering Don Juan are all here. And, with housing arrangements now in order, it is time "to make the proper observations." The observer replaces the participant: "The houses are all of clay and straw." There are more bloody banquets.[20]

While in Geesh, Bruce brings his medical skills to the villagers. He kills cattle "for the poor." He gives colored beads to girls of the village. But then he has to leave, and Irepone is disconsolate: "she tore her fine hair, which she had every day before braided in a newer and more graceful manner; she threw herself upon the ground in the house, and refused to see us mount on horseback, or take our leave, and came not to the door till we were already set out, then followed us with her good wishes and her eyes, as far as she could see or be heard." It is the classic film shot: Shane rids the valley of gunmen, then rides into the distance as Joey calls after him; Dido watches Aeneas sailing away and prepares her funeral pyre. Here at the moment of parting, Bruce becomes the observer of the participants, one of them himself. He had a cinematic gift.[21]

After the beautiful Irepone, then the beautiful Melectanea. On his way back to Gondar, Bruce stays at the home of a notorious brigand, Shalaka Welled Amlac, whom he has earlier treated for smallpox. Welled Amlac is absent at first but his wife, an "arrant hag," and his two sisters, both of them "really handsome," are there to welcome him. Of the two, Melectanea is "the most beautiful and graceful." The stage is set. As drinks are poured all around, Melectanea "took a particular charge of me, and I began to find the necessity of retiring and going to bed while I was still able." Obvious though the outcome will be, Bruce equivocates. It is the "invariable custom" of the country to establish "a relationship by sleeping with a near of kin," but he feigns reluctance and then repeats Swift's insinuating lines about his relationship with the too-ardent Esther Vanhomrigh, the woman he called Vanessa:

> But what success Vanessa met
> Is to the world a secret yet;
> Can never to mankind be told,
> Nor shall the conscious muse unfold.

This was too much for Swift's biographer, the Earl of Orrery: "It is impossible to read this cruel hint without great indignation against

33

the *conscious muse*." And Bruce, with a wink, nods in agreement: "Fye upon the conscious muse, says Lord Orrery, and fye, too, say I: —A man of honour and gallantry should not permit himself such a hint at this, though the Red Sea was between him and his mistress." There can be no doubt what happened, but conventions of honor and gallantry oblige Bruce to draw a thin veil, one more time, on the scene.[22]

When Bruce finally headed home late in 1771, Ozoro Esther surprised him by arranging a rendezvous to postpone his journey. It afforded them one last romantic idyll in the mountain village of Tcherkin. But after two happy weeks, Bruce resumed his journey, now through fierce desert heat, to the forbidding kingdom of Sennar, where once again his medical skills helped see him through. A local sheikh suffered from stomach disorders, perhaps brought on by excessive drinking, for which Bruce administered ipecac, not only to the sheikh but to the women of the court, who seem to have enjoyed the emetic experience. Most of them were very large and not at all the objects of Bruce's desire, but there was one exception. This was the beautiful Aiscach, who inspires Bruce to his most ardent raptures yet.

When the ipecac treatments are finished, he sees one of the women, veiled and robed, who now removes her veil down to her shoulders. A servant, "as in play, pulled off the remaining part of the veil that covered her." And, with all or much now revealed: "I was astonished at the sight of so much beauty." Her hair, ornamented with beads and cowrie shells, is braided and twisted about her head; she wears gold earrings and, around her neck, four rows of gold chain; her dress is a blue shift that "hung loosely about her, and covered her down to her feet, though it was not very rigorously nor very closely disposed all below her neck." The gaze of the proto-anthropologist pries its way through the loose blue shift. "Tallest of the middle size," Aiscach is not fifteen, her features so "faultless" that "they might have served alone for the study of a painter all his life, if he was in search of absolute beauty." After these raptures, we think we know what to expect next. But it doesn't happen. Or does it? More than ever before, Bruce leaves us guessing. As he is about to head off again, Aiscach cries out: "what are you going to do?" He answers: "I am going to do, Madam ... one of the most disagreeable things I ever did in my life; I am going to take leave of you." He is well schooled by now in the rituals and rhetoric of partings.[23]

Bruce was not quite forty when he arrived in Ethiopia. He was forty-three by the time he returned to London, after a spell in France and Italy, in summer, 1774. Soon he was an object of fun. Horace Walpole sneered at him and his stories. Johnson thought he was unreliable. Peter Pindar and Isaac Cruikshank took aim, and Bruce became a sensation, though not the sort he had hoped for. More accustomed as he was to tribal hostilities than the sniping of literary London, he fled to Kinnaird, his estate in Stirlingshire, not far from Bannockburn. He married again and had three children, two of whom survived him. When his wife died in 1785, friends prodded him into putting together his *Travels,* published in 1790.[24] In the end he grew enormously fat, sometimes adorning himself, as if in homage to the traveller he once had been, in "an eastern habit and turban." In April 1794, coming down the stairs at Kinnaird, he tripped, fell heavily to the ground, and died. Over time the authenticity of the *Travels* was slowly accepted and Bruce's reputation as a truthteller largely restored. Yet his greatest contribution, much like that of Samuel Johnson before him, may have been to fix Ethiopia's place in the British consciousness as a site of wonder.[25]

❖ MANSFIELD PARKYNS

In the first half of the nineteenth century, Ethiopia swarmed with British visitors—adventurers, artists, diplomats—and books came off the presses, on average, every six or seven years. The names of these early travellers do not figure large even in the annals of exploration: Henry Salt, Nathaniel Pearce, John Bell, Walter Plowden, William Cornwallis Harris, Charles Beke, Mansfield Parkyns—and others. But Samuel Johnson was right: "there has rarely passed a life of which a judicious and faithful narrative would not be useful." Salt, Pearce, Plowden, Harris, and Beke all published Ethiopian narratives and are not wholly lost to history. But Parkyns's story, thanks to the late Duncan Cumming's biography, is the most accessible. Himself a considerable figure in the history of Ethiopia and Eritrea at the time of their federation, Cumming unearthed, in Parkyns's story, a perfect counterpoint to that of the rampageous Scot, James Bruce. Cumming did not live to complete biographies he had planned of other early travellers, but his sketch of the unassuming Parkyns makes it evident that not every traveller-adventurer was cut from an identical piece of cloth.[26]

Bruce did not reach Abyssinia until he was in middle age; Parkyns arrived before he turned twenty. He had been sent down from Cambridge for some unrecorded prank. Like his companions, Bell and Plowden, who for a time travelled with him, he could have been an American college student, or Jack Kerouac, loose on the road; or any other young Briton on the Grand Tour, except that his tour eventually took him far beyond the precincts of Paris, Florence and Rome. The account that he published in 1853, *Life in Abyssinia*, had real virtues. Without effacing the image of Ethiopia as a wondrous destination, Parkyns let it be known that here was a land, despite its violence, where ordinary people could lead ordinary lives.

He also recognized, as others did not, that a personal narrative of travel and a survey of other peoples along the way are different undertakings. Finally he recognized, ahead of his time, that the concept of national character is no more than a useful fiction, at best; at worst, a calumny. But what he did not reveal, leaving it for Duncan Cumming to discover many years later, was the secret of his private life in this distant land.

Born in 1823, fifteen years before Victoria was crowned, Parkyns came from a well-to-do, quirky family in Nottinghamshire that represented, as Cumming puts it, "an English 'aristocratic' tradition of the raffish and red-blooded variety." To this raffish heritage, Parkyns added a life story of red-blooded, even shocking, adventure that coexisted with a sense of Victorian decorum. Lady Palmerston was shocked. Quoting Richard Lister Venables, another Victorian traveller, she described Parkyns's adventures as "the most successful attempt by a man to reduce himself to the savage state on record." Yet he became, when his travelling days were over, a village squire, a farmer, a somewhat reluctant civil servant, a doer of good deeds, and the father of nine children, one of whom, an only son, died in infancy. He is said to have taken a cold bath every day, "a reminder perhaps of the Spartan life on which he had thrived in his youth." Set besides so many self-regarding, if not megalomaniac, adventurers, Parkyns's temperate nature stands out. His acceptance of Victorian convention makes his secret story that much more compelling.[27]

After he was sent down from Cambridge, for whatever minor offense, he made the mandatory stops on the continental tour, and then, having met the eccentric Richard Monckton Milnes in the Greek islands, the two of them travelled together to Istanbul and to Egypt. Eventually, thoughts of Abyssinia and the Nile took hold of Parkyns, and the spring of 1843 found him in Massawa. For some three years he lived in the Ethiopian highlands and, after more assorted travels, returned to England in the summer of 1849. While in Ethiopia he turned himself into as much of an Ethiopian as perhaps it was possible to do: Venables was not wrong in his estimate of Parkyns—except that the "savage" state to which he was "reduced" could better be described as a thorough and successful adaptation to a different style of life from the one into which he had been born.

As he presents himself in *Life in Abyssinia,* Parkyns the traveller is no one special, unschooled as a writer, reluctant to enter on the public stage, even a naïf: "I offer the following pages to the public"—he began—"with some diffidence, though not with any feeling of regret for the style or composition; for I do not pretend to be learned in book-making." As an observer, he offers himself as the innocent truth-teller, telling it the way it was as best he can remember it, although sometimes, he concedes, he may have fallen into a "common error, that of putting down as customs, incidents which I may have seen, but which, in reality, may happen scarcely once in a hundred years." This disclaimer is advanced, it turns out, in defense of none other than James Bruce: "I make this remark on account of the reputation poor Bruce got." Has anyone besides the wide-eyed Mansfield Parkyns ever thought of his predecessor as "poor Bruce?" Granted, there is something disingenuous in all this, but an author should be allowed a public persona. Parkyns manages his persona with some skill, even if the reader could be forgiven for thinking every so often of the wide-eyed Lemuel Gulliver.[28]

While Parkyns comes to Bruce's defense, he will not, he says, be dealing in marvels himself—although he has heard, on good authority, that among the Galla tribes it is "not uncommon" to cut steaks from a live animal. To the charge that this is monstrous cruelty, Parkyns replies that crimping salmon and skinning eels are also cruel practices—not to mention the "horrible" deaths meted out to Royalists convicted of high treason in the days of Cromwell and the interregnum. When Parkyns says, "I haven't got any thing marvelous to tell—I wish I had," he is mindful that in human affairs little is so marvelous that equivalent examples can't be found as easily at home as abroad: cultural relativism is not new. It is the insight of the naïve observer-participant that makes possible a more sophisticated reading of ourselves. Gulliver understood many things that his fellow Europeans did not.[29]

Dressing the part is prerequisite to living it, and Parkyns abandoned his European clothes at first opportunity, giving them to a friend in a gesture of renunciation. "From the day I left Suez"—in March 1843—"till about the same time in the year 1849, I never wore any article of European dress.... I wore no covering to my head, except a little butter, when I could get it; nor to my feet, except the horny sole which a few months' rough usage placed under them." And, no matter the lack of hat and shoes: "During the whole of this time I never had a headache, though exposed to the sun all hours of the day, and was never footsore, though I walked constantly in the roughest imaginable places." Parkyns permits himself a touch of insider pride. Any European who can thrive without a hat in the African sun, walk barefoot over rough African terrain, or smear his uncovered head with butter, knows something that most Europeans do not. So does anyone whose diet has included "lion, leopard, wolf, cat, hawk, crocodile, snake, lizard, locust, &c." The "&c." invites us to wonder what the "cetera" could possibly have been. However diffident as an author, and later decorous as a village squire, Parkyns enjoyed tweaking European sensibilities.[30]

When it came time to write his story, however, he found himself with a question that the egotistical James Bruce would not have noticed: how to marry the demands of personal narrative, on the one hand, and an account of different people and their customs, on the other? Perhaps remembering Horace's injunction that a work of art should instruct or delight, Parkyns says at the start: "a book of travels should be either a scientific work or an entertaining one." And then: "It was my original intention to write solely on the habits of the people, without bringing myself into notice." For the reason that will come clear, Parkyns might have wanted to exclude his own story entirely, but his publisher (most likely) persuaded him otherwise: "I was … told that without a little personal narrative the book would be unreadable." Therefore: "I have … divided the subject into two parts—Travel, and Manners and Customs." The two parts are then allotted separately to the two volumes of *Life in Abyssinia*, a division that signals fair intentions even though it is impossible, except in a general way, to maintain. In an excess of his usual modesty, Parkyns disclaims success in either category, but his diffidence is again calculated. Beneath his "aw, shucks" air—in the North American vernacular—lay not only an overarching concern to do justice to Ethiopia but some understanding, stemming from the particulars of his own story, of narrative complications that he and every traveller-observer run up against.[31]

At the heart of the second volume on "manners and customs," following chapters that deal with "personal appearance, dress, &c.," "births and marriages, "deaths and funerals," and so on, comes a chapter with the bland title: "Anecdotes illustrative of character, etc." Once more, mildness of manner cloaks a tougher line of argument, this time about "the character of a nation," and Parkyns emerges with honors: "It is a difficult task," he says, "for any man to form a just opinion of the character of a nation…. Travellers are far too apt to attribute to an entire population traits which they may have observed in the townspeople, or even in their own immediate followers. Such an estimate is evidently unfair." When travellers "spoil the people with whom they come in contact," still more uncertainty creeps in, and a traveller's progress, "after the Manner of Hogarth," may end in "scene the last,—a totally false estimate of the nation's character." Parkyns admits that he too has probably erred, but "the longer a person remains in a country and the more he mixes with the natives and assimilates himself to them, which is of still greater importance, the less likely he is to form a false opinion of their dispositions." What Lady Palmerston thought was descent into a savage state, Parkyns calls "mixing with the natives" and "assimilation." This is his apologia, and it is well-earned.[32]

Even though he knew that assertions about national character or groups of individuals are no more than assertions about a majority or a collective average, Parkyns sometimes permits himself a harmless generality: "The fair sex all over the world are fond of ornaments. In Abyssinia they wear a profusion of silver." Sometimes he goes farther out on a limb: "no nation is more loudly Christian than the Abyssinians." But usually he adds a "most" or a "perhaps" or an appeal to other authority. He is careful with his data: "The Abyssinians are of middle stature, averaging I should think about 5 feet 7 inches, rather more than less." On one occasion, this habitual caution leads to genial excess. The subject is the very one that had often stirred James Bruce: "In feature, as in form, the young Abyssinian women are perhaps among the most beautiful on the earth." Not content with a precautionary "perhaps," Parkyns then attaches a footnote: "I have heard it remarked by a connoisseur that no women are to be compared to them but the French half-castes of the Mauritius." This is delicious. It takes an expert and a footnote to substantiate the beauty of Ethiopian women. Luckily for science, beauty here is confirmed in the eye of at least two beholders, one the amateur Parkyns, the other an expert connoisseur.[33]

But the amateur observer of beauty had an interest that he did not declare. At the heart of his travels, and of his first volume, is a nine-month stay in the remote mountain district of Rohabeita, over-looking the Mareb river valley in the northwest corner of the country: beyond, Duncan Cumming said, the back of beyond. It was Parkyns's own enchanted valley: "I look back on Rohabaita as a sort of 'Happy Valley,' with all the necessary enjoyments and none of the drawbacks of the one described by Johnson."[34] In this "wild spot" he spent many "happy hours." He delighted in the natural beauty and the wildlife, especially the birds. It was "one of the happiest periods" of his life. He became a "chief, or man of importance" and was "consulted on all important occasions"—most probably because, and this was his big unacknowledged secret, he took a wife; a secret that would have alarmed Lady Palmerston more than anything else she may have heard. Or maybe she did know, by rumor or report, as would help explain her belief that Parkyns had uniquely succeeded in reducing himself to a savage state. Like Bruce's women, Parkyns's wife, whose name was Tures, was high-born. All this Duncan Cumming, serving in Adwa, learned when he unearthed the story in 1941. He also learned that Parkyns and Tures had a child, a boy named John, later imprisoned by Emperor Tewodros and rescued at Maqdala by General Napier. Descendants of John Parkyns fled Ethiopia when Haile Selassie was deposed in the 1970s and came to London. In time, others of the family came to California.[35]

Of the marriage Parkyns said nothing in his book and very little in his private journal, also unearthed by Cumming. In one journal entry, however, Parkyns looks back fondly: "It was then"—at a bacchanal on St. Michael's day, full of drinking and dancing and the occasional fight but not (so far as we are told) the goings-on at Bruce's bloody banquet—"that I first met a friend whom I have had reason to forget, not a friend of a day but one whose attachment was tried through all my stay in Abyssinia … as a friend whose sincerity and attachment and as a servant whose devotion and fidelity might well set aside the prejudices which vain Europeans have against a skin a little darker than our own." Parkyns's sincere, devoted, faithful friend and servant was his wife Tures.[36]

In post-colonial times, we are made uneasy by an effusion like this or an alliance like that of Parkyns and Tures. Mary Louise Pratt lays out the complications of eros in a colonial world. "Sentimentality and *sensibilité*," she notes, "began asserting themselves in travel writing about the same time as science did, from the 1760s on." And, in this literature, "sex and slavery are great themes." The Scottish soldier/traveller John Stedman married a young slave in Surinam, a marriage that Pratt calls, "like many transracial affairs in the fiction of this time, … a romantic transformation of a particular form of colonial sexual exploitation"—that is, Europeans taking local women to serve as sexual and domestic partners. These stories end predictably: "the lovers are separated, the European is reabsorbed by Europe, and the non-European dies an early death." We do not know whether Tures died early or late, but her story matches the archetype: not only is she Parkyns's wife but his devoted servant.[37]

At the same time, what is true in the general is not always, or not equally, true in the particular. Who would get the better marks in any moral judgment: the roistering James Bruce or the decorous Mansfield Parkyns, whose marriage may have taken place because he didn't want to seem profligate; or the married German aristocrat, Prince Hermann von Pückler-Muskau, who bought an Ethiopian slave girl in Cairo in 1837, took her as his mistress, brought her to

Europe where she died of consumption at the age of sixteen, buried her in the family church, and, after her death, called her "the being I loved most of all the world;" not to mention Arthur Rimbaud, whose sojourn in Harar included alliances with two Ethiopian women, a case of syphilis, and an abiding affection for his young Harari manservant? It would take a skilful casuist to distribute praise or blame among these contrasting stories. The dilemma posed by the clash of general claims and particular instances was wonderfully expressed by Swift as he pondered his creation, Gulliver: "I hate and detest that animal called man, although I hartily love John, Peter, Thomas and so forth." The throw-away "and so forth" insinuates the sly knowledge that hating the tribe and loving the individual is an inescapable paradox in our thinking about the world. Mansfield Parkyns, ready enough to challenge European values but also a product of these values, would have been unhappy to know that he could be tarred with the colonial brush. In his lament for Tures, he credits himself with "the courage and prudence necessary to separate myself from scenes and persons rendered dear to me by long attachment." Affection for home and family is all that consoles him for having had to leave. But would he really have preferred to stay? The usual story of the colonist going out to India (or wherever) and, in the end, gladly returning gets a new twist. But nostalgia, among the vainest of human wishes, diminishes the present in favor of the past. Perhaps all we should say of the amiable Mansfield Parkyns is that he loved Ethiopia and then he came home.[38]

❖   RICHARD BURTON

In her biography of Rimbaud, who fled France and poetry and spent the last years of his life in and around Harar, Enid Starkie utters the biographer's *cri de coeur*: "All those who study Rimbaud soon reach a gulf of mystery which their imagination and intuition seem unable to bridge." No doubt the lament is truly felt, though it also sells books. And if it is more than ordinarily true of Rimbaud, the poet turned African trader, it is also more than ordinarily true of Richard Burton. In its remarkable opacity, his life—the real, mysterious story of it—holds biographers spellbound. The exaggerated tale that his wife Isabel destroyed all his papers after his death makes an abyss waiting to be filled with speculation.[39] But beyond the mystery of the conflagration, Burton himself made a career out of self-concealment. He was a gaudy, flamboyant figure but when it really counted, he gave almost nothing of himself away. Like other of his narratives, *First Footsteps in East Africa* (1856), in which his daring visit to Harar is the centerpiece, is crammed with facts delivered in a cool, "scientific" manner. Though he relished his role as the pilgrim Hajj Abdullah—the role he played when he went to Mecca and Medina—and though his comrades in arms in India sometimes called him the "white nigger," very little in Burton's history could be thought of, even by his most hostile antagonists (and there were many), as going native. He was too much a loner for that. His disguises were strategies, not acts of assimilation. He was protean in his abilities and roles, fluent in many languages, but through it all maintained a fierce reserve. Going native was precisely what he did not do. He watched, above the ebb and flow, no matter what the extent of his participation may have been. He had none of Bruce's roistering ways and nothing of Parkyns's sentimental streak. Richard Burton the observer was all business, sometimes frighteningly so.[40]

In a sense he does not quite belong here: at the time of his visit in 1855, the walled city of Harar was an autonomous city-state, one of Islam's holy places. Only in the 1890s during the reign of Menelik II, did Harar, near the Somali border and some two hundred miles from Addis Ababa, became part of "greater Ethiopia."[41] But Burton knew that his venture to Harar, from which he hoped to find his way to the sources of the White Nile, brought him into the realm of Lobo and of Bruce, even though Harar lay in the Islamic south, not in the Christian highlands.

The explorer's passion to be first, whether to Timbuctoo, to the sources of the Nile, or to the summit of Everest, ran at least as high in Burton as it had in Bruce, even though he cloaked desire in the objectivity of description and, for the most part, kept inner flames somewhere out of sight. He was first to reach Mecca, Medina, and then Harar. He hoped he would be first to reach the sources of the White Nile. His cool descriptions went hand in hand with motivations that were anything but cool, and his aggrandizing title, *First Footsteps in East Africa,* lets the genie of desire out of the bottle; German missionaries, as Burton knew, had set foot in much of East Africa decades before, and Ethiopia was hardly virgin land. But he has risked more than the others and has come away safe, unlike the unlucky Alexander Gordon Laing, murdered in 1826 after reaching Timbuctoo: "I doubt not there are many who ignore the fact that in Eastern Africa, scarcely three hundred miles distant from Aden, there is a counterpart of ill-famed Timbuctoo in the Far West." The journey from Aden to Harar does not match Laing's epic camel trek across the desert, some 1500 miles, from Tripoli to Timbuctoo, but the risks Burton ran were real: it would be death, he had been told, to enter the holy city. In daredevil fashion, he has succeeded where others—a mixed lot of diplomats, soldiers, missionaries, and wanderers, English, German, and French—have all failed: "The more adventurous Abyssinian travelers, Salt and Stuart, Krapf and Isenberg, Barker and Rochet—not to mention divers Roman Catholic

Missioners—attempted Harar, but attempted it in vain. The bigoted ruler and barbarous people threatened death to the Infidel who ventured within their walls.... Of all foreigners the English were, of course, the most hated and dreaded." Of course. Brought up in France as a boy, Burton was not very fond of his countrymen but was not averse to trading on English identity when it served him: not only does he overcome great danger, but the danger is greatest for him, an Englishman. In the event, he abandoned Arab dress in favor of his uniform as a British soldier to enter the city, realizing that his skin color would give him away. Abandoning his disguise probably gave him as much pleasure as did the disguise itself: if the English were the most hated and dreaded of foreigners, then it should be an Englishman who conquers Harar. And better an Englishman than a Scot—like James Bruce.[42]

Bruce arouses in Burton the same combative spirit that damaged, beyond repair, his relations with his equally combative companion John Hanning Speke, whose claim to have identified the source of the Nile in Lake Victoria infuriated Burton beyond reason. For the account he gives of Ethiopian history, Father Lobo is Burton's principal source and, he says, "I love the style of this old father." In fact, the style that Burton loves seems to be Samuel Johnson's: a mistranslation from the Somali that Burton attributes to Lobo is Johnson's mistranslation of his French original.[43] But mistranslation is a minor transgression compared to the far more grievous sins, as Burton saw them, of James Bruce: "I love the style of this old father, so unjustly depreciated by our writers, and called ignorant peasant and liar by Bruce, because he claimed for his fellow countrymen the honour of having discovered the Coy Fountains. The Nemesis who never sleeps punished Bruce by the justest of retributions. His pompous and inflated style, his uncommon arrogance, and overweening vanity, his affectation of pedantry, his many errors and mis-representations, aroused against him a spirit which embittered the last years of his life." Then Burton remembers, it may be, the good-natured Mansfield Parkyns and his defence of Bruce: "It is now the fashion to laud Bruce, and to pity his misfortunes. I cannot but think that he deserved them." This is harsh. Burton never felt much pity for anybody, and he must have thought of Parkyns as insufficiently hardened for the rough and tumble contact sport of exploration and discovery. Through Burton's assault runs an undercurrent of unde-fined feeling, jealousy perhaps or its alter-ego, resentment.[44]

However impulsive and difficult Richard Burton may have been in his relationships with others, none could doubt his almost preternatural powers of attention and description, even at moments of great stress and even when, as in Harar, he had to go outside the city walls before putting pen to paper. On entering Harar, he is brought before the Amir, "a bigoted prince whose least word was death." But if we take him at his word, the presence of danger does not diminish Burton's ability to register everything that comes before his eye. The Amir's throne room, dark with whitewashed walls, is hung with "significant decorations—rusty matchlocks and polished fetters." He gives the appearance "of a little Indian Rajah, an etiolat-ed youth twenty-four or twenty-five years old, plain and thin-beard-ed, with a yellow complexion, wrinkled brows and protruding eyes." And his dress is "a flowing robe of crimson cloth, edged with snowy fur, and a narrow white turband tightly twisted round a tall conical cap of red velvet, like the old Turkish headgear of our painters." Before the advent of photography, explorers took sketch pads with them on their travels; Burton himself sketched the Amir, as if to con-firm his verbal picture. But the verbal picture is finely detailed. Suddenly we imagine the Amir in his headgear looking like Hogarth, done up *à la Turque*. Henry James once said—and he blamed the "picture magazine" especially—that the Anglo-Saxon mind had lost the faculty of attention. Not many observers, before Burton or after, have matched his skill in seeing whatever lay before his eyes.[45]

The same cool intensity of observation is everywhere. The women of Harar, "beautiful by contrast with their lords," have "small heads, regular profiles, straight noses, large eyes, mouths approaching the Caucasian type, and light yellow complexions." They are also very loud: "The female voice is harsh and screaming, especially when heard after the delicate organs of the Somal." What distinguishes Burton, here, from comparable moments in Bruce and Parkyns: we cannot tell, and Burton wanted it this way, whether his own feelings are in any way engaged, sexually or otherwise. The uncertainty surrounding his sexuality is largely the product, here and in everything he wrote, of more than scrupulous detachment. The women of Harar may be beautiful in their way, but only "by contrast with their lords." The women of Somalia may speak softly, but it is their "organs" that are delicate, as if their soft voices were detachable from themselves. When Burton permits himself a less austere moment, it involves no less detachment, only a momentary irony: the "freedom of manners" among Harari women "renders a public flogging occasionally indispensable," a flogging that is then made vivid by the observer's unflinching gaze: "Before the operation begins, a few gourds full of cold water are poured over their heads and shoulders, after which a single-thonged whip is applied with vigour." The water is cold, the whip is single-thonged, and Burton looks on like a spectator in a surgical amphitheater. James Bruce and Mansfield Parkyns were amateurs by comparison, both of them subject to simple passions and pleasures of the flesh.[46]

"Anthropology," like so much else, was a nineteenth-century

invention, and Burton had a hand in its creation, both its name and its practice. In 1863, he and James Hunt founded the Anthropological Society of London, later merged with the Royal Anthropological Institute of Great Britain and Ireland. But even more important than the name that became attached to this new science was Burton's practice in the field—with its astonishing combination of antisepsis and intimacy. Never, perhaps, has there been so intimate a recorder of sexual behavior, from the time he investigated the male brothels of Karachi to his final disquisition on the "sotadic zone."⁴⁷ Often we have no idea at all of how he knew what he claimed to know. Some things it seems he could have known only by participation. How otherwise did he know that Galla women had vaginal muscles that could induce orgasm merely by their contractions? Some things he describes so vividly as to imply first-hand observation, even when that seems unlikely. The husband of an infibulated Somali woman, we are told, if unable to overcome "the blockage with his sword of love," resorts to bloody violence: "[H]e opens the pudendum from the lower end with a knife and immediately thrusts his penis up through the bloody opening." Some other things he might have known by participation or observation or report, for example, that "[t]he Somalis have only one method of making love. Both parties lie on their sides, never, as is our custom, the man on the woman. The woman lies on her left side, the man on his right...." We have no idea whether, or to what degree, Burton depended on informants, watched on the sidelines, or participated firsthand. Nor, for that matter, can we be sure that he didn't make some of it up; the anthropological terrain, like that of any traveller, offers rich possibilities of fabulation.⁴⁸

The convention that governed anthropology for its first century and a half, that the anthropologist has no evident sexual identity, marked Burton's reporting from the start. Taught by their professional superiors to be "a fly on the wall" or to "assume the pose of a little child" in their fieldwork, anthropologists have paid tribute to Burton's ghost. Only in the last few decades has the ideal of perfect sexual neutrality in the field been exposed as a fiction and "the silence enshrouding sex in the field" been broken.[49] Burton's own silence has never been penetrated. Mansfield Parkyns was also silent though his happiness welled over him. James Bruce was anything but silent. I think that is one reason why Burton disliked Bruce so much. He violated rules and practices that Burton, perhaps with Bruce in mind, would do much to initiate.[50]

If we know nothing for sure about how Burton acquired his store of sexual information, we do know, more trivially, that he participated in the daily ritual in Yemen and Harar, unchanged to the present, of chewing leaves of the mildly narcotic qat. Not only did he participate, he thought himself something of a connoisseur. About this aspect of everyday life, the anthropologist could be open: "I could not but remark the fine flavour of the plant after the coarser quality grown in Al-Yemen." The qat ceremony that he describes takes place in the company of local grandees, and the chief councillor seats Burton, "after polite inquiries," at his right hand on the dais. In this position of honor, Burton strikes a magisterial pose and, as participant-observer, gives us an observing look at himself. "I ate Kat and fingered my rosary." No doubt the rosary is Islamic, but the contrasting associations of European Catholicism crowd in. Then Burton helps untangle for the company a textual crux in a Muslim blessing. The European chewing qat, fingering a rosary, and explicating an Arabic text is the cosmopolitan figure that Burton wanted the world to know. Even so, Lawrence's image of himself as one suspended between two worlds, like Mohammed's coffin, is apt.[51]

Despite its dangers, Harar was in some ways too easy a triumph. Burton strode into the city with his mules and found himself facing a ruler whose sickly appearance was at odds with his reputation and whose pale smile signaled that all would be well. In ten days Burton recorded the sights and sounds and smells and climate and history of Harar as well as the outlines of its language. Even so, he was bored: "Our days at Harar were monotonous enough." And, leaving the city, he experiences the same sort of depression that afflicted Bruce after reaching the Blue Nile: "I had time, on the top of my mule for musing upon how melancholy a thing is success. Whilst failure inspirits a man, attainment reads the sad prosy lesson that all our glories 'are shadows, not substantial things.'" The implacable Richard Burton has let his guard down, but not for long: "The shade of melancholy soon passed away. The morning was beautiful. A cloudless sky, then untarnished by sun, tinged with reflected blue the mist-crowns of the distant peaks and the smoke wreaths hanging round the sleeping villages, and the air was a cordial after the rank atmosphere of the town. The dew hung in large diamonds from the coffee trees...." After the sad, prosy, and ancient lesson that human wishes are vain, the poetic skies of early morning, reflected blues, distant peaks, and wreaths of smoke restore Burton to himself, much as the cool night air rescued Bruce from his melancholy fit.[52]

After Burton's successful venture to Harar, Ethiopia soon became less an exotic destination, more a counter in the games of empire. Only in the 1930s would there be another Abyssinian explorer, Wilfred Thesiger, in the tradition of Bruce and Burton. And Thesiger was something of a throwback. By 1930, when Haile Selassie was crowned, Ethiopia was being swept along by political currents and partisan struggles of the modern world.

INTERLUDE: *Maqdala*

B URTON S JOURNEY TO HARAR marked a turning point: no longer isolated, Ethiopia now participated in the wider world. When the Emperor Tewodros took members of the British diplomatic colony and others of the European community captive at Maqdala in the 1860s—he was offended to have received no reply to a letter he had sent Queen Victoria—it generated a crisis. The prisoners were held captive for four years until an expeditionary force, under command of General Sir Robert Napier, later first Baron Napier of Magdala, landed at Massawa, traversed hundreds of difficult miles, and eventually freed them in 1868. Learning of the defeat, Tewodros committed suicide.

Back in England, the plight of the captives and the fortunes of the expeditionary force were the topic of the day. Among the correspondents who covered Napier's campaign were G.A. Henty and Henry Stanley.[1] *The Illustrated London News* feasted on the story for months and, when it was all over, published a long account of the expedition with a gathering of illustrations that had appeared in its pages.[2] Books tumbled from the press. And John Camden Hotten, an enormously energetic publisher who always kept his eye on the main chance—he published Blake, Swinburne, Whitman, Baudelaire and other notables as well as a *History of Signboards* (1866) and a "particular line" of flagellation literature— seized the moment with an edited volume of his own, *Abyssinia and Its People; or, Life in the Land of Prester John.* Part anthology and part commentary, it is a field guide to everything Abyssinian, with extracts from Lobo, Bruce, Parkyns and other travellers both English and French; a short and shaky glossary of Abyssinian words "in frequent use;"[3] a bibliography, with something near 200 entries, of "works relating to Abyssinia," plus a request for "particulars of any works, the titles of which may have been omitted;" a line drawing of a menacing and outsize "tzetseai" fly—even though, as Hotten reports, Abyssinia is not actually infested with this "terrible fly;" and, foremost, considerations of the crisis at Maqdala. Tipped in at the front (in the Stanford University Libraries' copy) is an advertisement for a "new popular book on Abyssinia," *A Visit to King Theodore, by a Traveller Lately Returned from Gondar,* also published by Hotten. The frontispiece to *Abyssinia and Its People,* one of several crude illustrations, shows—no surprise—a squatting Abyssinian "devouring raw beef." The plight of the captives had generated a whole new field of journalistic attention .[4]

What Hotten emphasizes in his text is not so much raw beef and tsetse flies as the new familiarity of this exotic land, subject to so many a sigh of wonder yet, by 1868, neither an unknown nor an unknowable place. On 9 October 1867, while the crisis was on, the *Times* had editorialized: "It is almost a truism to say that the better a country is known, the more difficult it is to write a book about it. Just now we know very little of Abyssinia, and therefore a dull book, provided it contains trustworthy facts concerning that region, would be read with eagerness." Hotten sets out to provide facts, and one of them, as he points out, is that facts are no longer hard to come by. Abyssinia has become more like a strange land next door: "A great deal of nonsense has of late been written about the appalling dangers of Abyssinia, and the extreme difficulties of travelling there under any and all circumstances, and one object of this volume was to show with what comparative ease (all things considered) several travellers—some very indifferently equipped—have passed through almost every part of the country." All quite true, but Tewodros, the very troublesome emperor, was a figure dangerous enough to stir the imagination of those who were safe at home in their beds.[5]

Hotten's character of the emperor is a small classic of Victorian portraiture, adapted to the taste of those who liked their savages with at least a touch of nobility. He supplants crude racial stereotypes in the English press with a savage partly noble, partly crazed: "Six months ago he was generally spoken of as a mere remove from an orang-outang.... One of the latest exhibitions of this ignorance is the cartoon of *Punch*, where the Abyssinian monarch is represented as a negro of the lowest type, with flat nose and huge lips, attired in left-off top boots, and a military coat from Monmouth Street"—in Covent Garden, home to the rag trade—"a kind of music-hall Jim Crow, crouching and yelping at the feet of Lord Stanley, or somebody else, who presents him with an ultimatum on the point of a bayonet." But Ethiopia is not a land for Jim Crow caricatures, nor is Tewodros a contemptible ruler, no matter how *Punch* may have portrayed him: rather, he is "[b]rave and daring to a fault—untruthful and tricky over trifles; forgetful of self as an anchorite, and exacting of others in the extreme in all matters of obeisance and ceremony; chivalrous and forgiving one day, inhumanly cruel and bloodthirsty the next." In other words, a king of oriental romance, worthy to be Britain's enemy, even though he should "be deposed as soon as possible."[6]

In 1868 Hotten published still another volume of Abyssinian interest, though different in kind: this was *Views in Central Abyssinia*, photolithographs of sketches in the Semien highlands by a German artist Eduard Zander, with preface and commentary by a young English woman, Sophie Frances Fane Veitch. It is an unlikely-seeming combination of publisher, artist, and editor—Hotten, Zander and Veitch—but it brings a step or two out of the shadows, in the person of Sophie Veitch, a Victorian literary woman little known today but of some standing in her own time. This was her first appearance on the literary scene, and, like so much else in the 1860s, it was occasioned by the Maqdala episode.

How did young Sophie Veitch happen to bring into public view the sketches of Eduard Zander? He was an artist whose name she did not know and whose monogram she misinterpreted as "T.E." rather than "E.Z.", not an implausible reading but one suggesting some haste in assembling the collection for the press. Zander's original sketchbook recently turned up at the British Library, and the last of the drawings (portraying a curious badger-like animal) includes his signature in full.[7] While Veitch translates the artist's own, lengthy comments on his drawing, she does not notice his signature. The title page of her collection reads: *Views in Central Abyssinia with Portraits of the Natives of the Galla Tribes*— the portraits include one of the Galla woman whom Zander had married— *Taken in pen and ink under circumstances of peculiar difficulty, by T.E., a German traveller, believed at present to be one of the captives there. With descriptions by Sophie F. F. Veitch.* The dedication, by permission, is "To Her Most Gracious Majesty, the Queen." In the preface, we learn that "[t]hese interesting views of the highlands of Abyssinia are from sketches made, in the years 1853–54, by a German artist, and subsequently sent as a present to the Anglican Bishop in Jerusalem by Mr. Waldmeyer, one of his lay misionaries in Abyssinia, and now, unfortunately a captive there." The preface concludes by announcing that "[t]he orthography has been accommodated

throughout, as nearly as possible, to that of the War Office map."
Not only, then, do we wonder about Sophie Veitch but about others
in the story, the Anglican Bishop of Jerusalem, Waldmeier, Zander,
and also about Veitch's access to War Office maps.

Some answers, so far as I have been able to put them together,
are clear; others, inferential or speculative. In 1868, the Anglican-
German Bishopric of Jerusalem, a creation of the 1840s, was in the
charge of Bishop Samuel Gobat, Swiss-born and a hard-working
missionary in Abyssinia during the 1830s. Theophilus Waldmeier, as
Sophie Veitch reports, was a German missionary, captive at Maqdala.
Eduard Zander was an adventurer and artist who had been in
Abyssinia since the 1840s and taken a native wife; he too was at
Maqdala, and died soon afterwards, but he was not imprisoned.
That he knew Waldmeier is therefore certain, and he could at any
time have given him the sketchbook.[8] But how did Sophie Veitch
enter the picture?

The answer: her father was William Douglas Veitch, chaplain
to the Bishop of Jerusalem, but resident in London since 1862 as
curate of St. Saviour's Parish, Paddington.[9] So we can imagine a scenario like this: Eduard Zander, having by the 1860s fallen out of contact with the world he left behind him, nonetheless hopes to make a
mark in his European homeland and, with that in mind, gives his
sketches to Waldmeier for transmission to Bishop Gobat, knowledgeable about Ethiopia and in a position of authority to dissemi-
nate Zander's work. Having received the sketchbook, Gobat thinks
of his chaplain in London, where obsession with Maqdala is at fever
pitch. When the manuscript arrives in Douglas Veitch's hands, he
decides that his young, talented daughter Sophie is right for the job.
Between them, they sign on John Camden Hotten, ever on the lookout for new material about Abyssinia. And, with this hot new prop-

erty on their hands, they receive permission to dedicate the volume to the Queen.

Even if this scenario happens to be roughly accurate, it leaves other matters open: in particular, were Douglas Veitch and his daughter ever in Abyssinia themselves? Perhaps not: the "descriptions" that accompany Zander's sketches indicate that Sophie Veitch was versed in the travels of Bruce and Parkyns but not that she necessarily knew the country firsthand. Nor would she have absolutely needed to. With her native aptitude, a knowledge of the literature, and access to the War Office maps for help with geography and topography, she could without much trouble have achieved an air of close familiarity with the Abyssinian scene, though her descriptions of native vegetation and peasant dwellings seem at times to imply direct acquaintance. Whether her access to the War Office maps was the result of a special dispensation is unknown, but the maps themselves, no doubt compiled by earlier travelers on diplomatic and military missions, would have been indispensable at a time of the Maqdala engagement. Sophie Veitch's access to and reliance on the maps associate this simple gathering of highland scenes with the tumultuous history of Tewodros and of Maqdala.

In her subsequent career as a novelist, which lasted thirty years or more, Sophie Veitch achieved more than a little success. Her themes were Scotland—her family came from Dumfries—and religion and romance. Her first novel, *Wise as a Serpent* appeared the year after *Views in Central Abyssinia*. Her best-known, *The Dean's Daughter* (1888), garnered praise, in a vein characteristic of an age that reveled in enumerating great writers and great books and best books: "Recalls to some extent the vanished hand of the author of Jane Eyre …. 'The Dean's Daughter' firmly establishes Miss Veitch's position among the upper ten of the female novelists of the day."

Her *James Hepburn, Free Church Minister* (1888) inspired some thoughts of George Eliot: "Miss Veitch has a distinct and eloquent style.... Her method is the method of George Eliot, and she does not suffer by the comparison...." Veitch translated a Norse saga from a version by the Germanist Felix Dahn. In the 1880s, she wrote essays and reviews, often marked by some strong opinions, for a short-lived periodical, *The Scottish Review.* Hers was a Victorian career of considerable reach, and the Maqdala episode was its starting point.[10]

When the Maqdala captives were released, it brought great rejoicing. In the annals of empire, however, it is a matter of note that General Napier and his forces did not remain as conquerors but instead packed up and went home. The orphan son of the emperor, Prince Alamayou, was taken to England under protection of the Queen, photographed on the isle of Wight by Julia Margaret Cameron, eventually enrolled in Rugby School and, dying at the age of eighteen of pleurisy and despair, buried in St. George's Chapel, Windsor.[11] The strangeness of it all surpasses any of Sophie Veitch's fictions that followed after she introduced herself, by way of Maqdala, to the public world.

The following illustrations are from Sophie F. F. Veitch, Views in Central Abyssinia (1868), *courtesy Department of Special Collections, Stanford University Libraries. In the original printing, sketches and descriptions are on facing pages, descriptions to the left, sketches to the right.*

No. 2.—VIEW OF TANNEMORA, LOOKING SOUTH.

In this sketch one of the peculiar features of the Abyssinian Mountains begins to be apparent, in those flat plains, on the very summits of the hills, which have, in some instances, played no unimportant part in the stormy history of Abyssinia. Far bolder specimens of this formation will be seen in subsequent sketches.

The flat mountain plain in the present view is at an elevation of 9,400 feet above the level of the sea, and the huts planted on the very summit of these Alpine heights speak for the hardy physique of the Abyssinian race, and well agree with a fact mentioned by the present Anglican Bishop in Jerusalem, as noticed by him during his many years' residence in Abyssinia —that the natives would frequently sleep in the open air when there was frost on the ground, with absolutely no further covering than a piece of cotton cloth round their shoulders.

Beyond the farthest height the southern declivity of the Semien Mountains begins.

No. 5.—BRANCH OF THE ABARA, NEAR THE TACAZZY.

An interesting combination of both the mountain and river scenery of the province of Semien. These rivers are often beautiful, but, alas! treacherous. The larger ones abound in fish, but such rivers as the Tacazzy are likewise less pleasantly inhabited by crocodiles, and very dangerous, except just in the dry season, in consequence of the deep holes and whirlpools so common in them. Mr. Mansfield Parkyns has given a sad account of such dangers, resulting in the loss of one of his party while crossing the Tacazzy; and an amusing one of the treachery of one of the smaller streams inviting the weary travelers, by its bank of smooth clean sand, to rest, only to find themselves, soon after midnight, reposing, not peacefully, in six inches of water—the consequence of little more than a heavy shower among the hills above.

No. 17.—VIEW NEAR MAI TSALO.

The flat-topped mountain in this sketch presents a bolder instance than either of the former ones, of the natural rock fortresses of Abyssinia. Among the most famous are the Amba Gideon and the Amba Hay in the Semien Mountains, Debra Libanos in Shoa, and Mount Geshen, on the confines of Amhara, and Begemder.

Debra Libanos is the seat of a famous monastery. Mount Geshen was the fortress chosen after the massacre of Debra Damo as the scene of the imprisonment of the royal family, until they shared the same fate there at the hands of a Mohammedan chief, after which this strange custom seems to have been discontinued.

No. 29.—WEST SIDE OF CHINFARA, A SINGLE BRANCH
OF BEROCH WAHA.

This scene is rather further south than the last. Mount Chinfara is one
of the most extraordinary, in shape at least, of the Semien Mountains. It
consists of three peaks—the two seen in the sketch and a third, unfortunately not visible from the artist's point of view. Its height is not mentioned,
but the War Office map gives it as 10,840 feet.

No. 31.—CONTINUATION OF ABARA, TO THE RIGHT.

Just such a spot, as this lofty summit of Abara, must have been the scene of a story told to Mr. Mansfield Parkyns, and which may point a moral for all lovers of good cheer. It was held in charge for a certain chief by some monks who, having accumulated treasure, were disinclined to reinstate the rightful owner. Force was useless; the monks had only to draw up their rope and laugh at those below. But the pious monks loved good cheer, so the chief persuaded them to let him come up, with only one attendant, to visit them. Then it seemed that his people below had a fine fat cow desirable for a banquet, and various other good things such as the holy fathers loved. So up came one or two more attendants with the cow, and yet more with other good things, and while the chief and the monks employed themselves in feasting, his attendants employed themselves in drawing up their comrades. At last, when the feast was over, the worthy monks found they had paid as dear for their short-lived pleasures as Esau, and had only the alternative offered them by their guests of retiring unresistingly by the rope, or resistingly over the precipice without it.

No. 39.—A GALLA FROM LIMA.

This sketch, the last of the figure subjects, is certainly the most interesting of them all. On the portrait of this bright-eyed, intelligent-looking
Galla, with her flowing drapery folded so closely round her, more care has
eveidently been bestowed than on any other sketch—a fact accounted for
by a note at the foot of the sketch, in the artist's own hand, "A Galla from
Lima—now my wife."

CHAPTER THREE

Barbaric Splendors and Golden Legends: Wilfred Thesiger, Evelyn Waugh, Sylvia Pankhurst

The memory of Tewodros has lingered on, and a San Francisco romance writer—the sort whose signature style is bodice-ripping—recently made him the subject of a novel, *The Four Quarters of the World* (2006): "Tewodros was an incredibly magnetic and dynamic ruler," Karen Mercury gushed, "I developed a hate/love thing with him." So does her hero, an American adventurer named Ravinger Howland, modeled on none other than Richard Burton, "the sexiest, most testosterone-driven hero of all time;" and her heroine, one Dr. Delphine Chambliss, also American, loved by both Howland and Tewodros. The novel, dedicated to "Sir Richard F. Burton, the brave, bold bandit," contains "enough white-hot sex for those not faint of heart"—and also, it is claimed in a press release, offers a "historically accurate, and exciting new take on the classic story of Emperor Tewodros of Abyssinia." Just what is historically accurate in *The Four Quarters of the World* and what constitutes a new interpretation of history are not easy to guess. But Karen Mercury's Tewodros comes from the same white-hot imaginings as John Camden Hotten's "exceedingly crafty" emperor, who would have been at home in the pages of *The Arabian Nights*. His land, in Karen Mercury's fervent imagination, is a "barbaric and breathtaking kingdom." Barbaric and breathtaking kingdoms are always a draw.[1]

After Tewodros's death, the Italians took over Eritrea, and Menelik II came to the Ethiopian throne in 1889, handing the Italians a humiliating defeat at Adwa, in 1896, that was still smarting in Mussolini's day. Before and after Menelik's death in 1913, aspirants to the throne jockeyed for position. In 1916, the insurgent Ras Tafari defeated the forces of the then-current ruler Lij Iyasu and his father, Ras Mikael, in a victory at Sagale, consolidating his power and finally, in 1930, being crowned Emperor Haile Selassie, "Conquering Lion of the Tribe of Judah, King of Kings and Elect of God." One of Haile Selassie's considerable talents was self-publicity, and his coronation, as he had planned, turned all eyes to his corner of the world. He understood the allure of imperial display—the more spectacular, the better. In 1923 the diplomat Charles Fernand Rey had closed an introduction to *Unconquered Abyssinia,* one of his several books on Ethiopia, with a nostalgic hope that after the modernization that was coming, "some of the old atmosphere will be left to remind one of the barbaric splendour of 2000 years ago." Haile Selassie did everything he could to encourage that hope.[2]

❖ WILFRED THESIGER

Ras Tafari's victory at the battle of Sagale was the occasion of a grand triumphal procession. Among the spectators was the head of the British legation in Addis Ababa, Wilfred Thesiger, along with his family, including two young sons, Billy—the second Wilfred Thesiger—and Brian. After the celebrations were over, the elder Thesiger wrote to his mother in rhapsodic tones: "More cavalry came by and then three principal generals, in chains and dressed like the Negus, but each carrying on his shoulder a large stone as a mark of servitude. They came before the tent and prostrated themselves on the ground before following their chief to prison…. It was the most wonderful sight I have ever seen, wild and barbaric to the last degree, and the whole thing so wonderfully staged and orderly." He added that his sons, Billy (who was six) and Brian (who was five), "were thrilled and should never forget it." In that he was right, at least so far as Billy was concerned. Young children are anxious not to forget what their fathers would like them to remember.[3]

"Even now," Billy Thesiger wrote, "nearly seventy years later, I can recall almost every detail: the embroidered caps of the drummers decorated with cowries; a man falling off his horse as he charged by; a small boy carried past in triumph—he had killed two men though he seemed little older than myself." These, the sharpest of the younger Wilfred Thesiger's memories, are all in their way boyish things: drummers' caps, a man falling off his horse, a boy like himself carried in triumph. But then these vignettes combine with grander memories of Troy: "I had been reading *Tales from the Iliad.* Now, in boyish fancy, I watched the likes of Achilles, Ajax and Ulysses pass in triumph with aged Priam, proud even in defeat." To the events of that childhood day in 1916, Thesiger attributed longings that stayed with him for the rest of his life: "I believe that day implanted in me a life-long craving for barbaric splendour, for savagery and colour and the throb of drums."[4]

Explorers and adventurers often do not take well to formal schooling, sometimes rebelling, sometimes going along until something more engaging comes up. The young Edward Wortley Montagu was a perpetual truant. Bruce, Parkyns, and Burton all shared a haphazard and troubled education. Bruce went to Harrow but was chronically ill and, when he briefly studied law at Edinburgh, aged sixteen, his illness ended a career for which he would have been unsuited. Parkyns spent less than a year at Trinity College, Cambridge, before his rustication. Burton, at Trinity College, Oxford, found himself often out of place and finally succeeded in giving enough offense to get himself expelled—another in the line, including Edward Gibbon, of those who found little to encourage their talents at the university. No two people can ever have been less alike than Burton and Gibbon, but they shared, while at Oxford, a frustrated desire to study Arabic and a disdain for the donnish society they found there. Wilfred Thesiger, by contrast, was inclined not to protest but to take things as they came and wait his chance.

When it was time for the Thesiger family to return to England, young Billy was dismayed: "I could not believe we were really leaving Abyssinia." In his strange new setting, he became as English as he possibly could, just as, in later years, he dressed the part of the well-tailored banker with bowler hat and tightly rolled umbrella while he was in London. He went to a preparatory school, St. Aubyns, where the sadistic headmaster was even more sadistic than others of the breed. While there, his father died young, as had James Bruce's father and Mansfield Parkyns's. Then he went to Eton and liked it well enough. Tough in body and mind, he became a boxer. Then it was on to Magdalen College, Oxford, where—unlike Burton and Parkyns—he thrived, but not as a scholar. His Oxford was Matthew Arnold's: dreaming spires, choirboys singing, punting on the river. Eventually he received a third-class degree in modern history. In his last year he captained the boxing team. But all the while he yearned for the landscape he had left behind as a boy. Unlike Bruce and Parkyns and Burton, who were on the run from England, Wilfred Thesiger was always looking for the road home.[5]

His family's friendship with Ras Tafari opened the way. While he was in London in 1924, the future emperor invited Thesiger's mother to tea. She brought the boy with her, and he was dazzled by the slightly built visitor with the "sensitive and finely moulded face," beautifully robed in a "black, gold-embroidered silk coat." More dazzling was the coronation in 1930, which Thesiger attended on invitation to represent his late father: "The Coronation was the most stirring and impressive show I have ever seen. You could easily imagine yourself back in the days of Sheba." And yet, amidst all the pomp and circumstance—lion's mane crowns and velvet cloaks, drums and chanting and dancing—Thesiger recognized that there was a comic aspect to it all, that the splendour teetered on the edge of an illusion. At the triumph of Sagale, he had realized that the spell was at risk when someone fell off his horse. At the coronation, the Abyssinian diplomats wore European dress and cocked hats, "which was a pity;" a fly-over by the "Abyssinian air force" was missing two out of six planes because of recent crashes; the emperor's grand exit was spoiled because the carriage horses were "unmanageable"; and a huge fireworks display fizzled when, by an "unfortunate" accident, "they all went off at once." It could be Monty Python. For really authentic barbarism and really authentic splendor, Thesiger knew he needed to push further. But where?[6]

While in Addis Ababa for the coronation, he put the question to a member of the British diplomatic corps, Colonel Robert Cheesman, later the author of *Lake Tana and the Blue Nile* (1938) and himself an explorer. Thesiger's biographer Alexander Maitland records Cheesman's memory of the moment, charming in its recollection of Thesiger's young innocence: "I want to do some exploring," he said. "Is there anywhere I could go?" To which Cheesman replied that it was late in the exploring game and not much was left but the polar regions (and he had already claimed Lake Tana for himself).

Thesiger answered that he was not interested in cold places, and Cheesman "then reminded him that there was a nice hot spot down in the Danakil desert and that nobody had explored it to find out where the Awash river went to." Others had been to Danakil country, but Cheesman was correct: no one had tried to follow the Awash to its destination. Three years later, having graduated from Oxford, Thesiger set off for Danakil country.[7]

As geographical puzzles go, the question of where a river ends is less thrilling than where a river starts. And the Awash, some 500 miles long, is no match for the Nile or the Niger. The allure of the Danakil owed very little to the geography of the Awash—it ends in a desolate lake in northeastern Ethiopia, as Thesiger would discover—and almost everything to the dangers of the journey, which were great. When asked by the mother of a potential fellow traveller if the venture would be dangerous, Thesiger replied that it would and that "that was the point of doing it." To his exasperation, Peter Scott's mother said, "I am sorry, Mr. Thesiger, but in view of the risk I cannot possibly consent to my son coming with you."[8]

The Danakil tribesmen were, famously, warriors for whom "all that mattered … was to kill," who routinely castrated their victims, and who were said to wear their victims' testicles around their wrists. In the event, however, Thesiger found the reality of the Danakil different from their reputation: "I thought the Danakil an attractive-looking people, and despite their murderous reputation they appeared to manifest a genuine friendliness." To be sure, they "invariably castrated any man or boy whom they killed or wounded, removing both the penis and the scrotum," but the report that they wore their victims' testicles around their wrists was not true: "I never came across an instance of this, though I encountered a number of individuals who had just killed someone." Instead, "the trophy is exhibited round the village and then thrown away." All this rather jolly killing, Thesiger decides, is a type of blood sport, the sort of thing that the British, of all people, ought to understand: "I was prepared to accept the fact that that they would kill a man or boy with as little compunction as I would shoot a buck. Their motive would be much the same as that of an English sportsman who visited Africa to shoot a lion." And the decorations of the Danakil—ostrich feathers, slit ears, colored loin cloths, bracelets, and daggers—are merely campaign medals like those of a British soldier who has fought in Crimea or the Ardennes. Like Parkyns, Thesiger raises the dodgy question of cultural relativism, this time in a context more acute than that of cruelty to oxen. There cannot be many moments in the history of anthropology, or travel writing generally, when the question has been more starkly posed. Fifty years ago, Ruth Benedict's *Patterns of Culture* (1946) was an almost mandatory text for undergraduates, and it enshrined the doctrine of cultural relativism among several cohorts of students. Nothing in the Kwakiutl culture of the North American northwest or the pueblo culture of the American southwest, however, carries such (let's say) visceral impact as the Danakil habit of triumphal killing and taking as trophies "both the penis and the scrotum." The fact that these trophies, in Thesiger's account, are not worn about the wrist but eventually thrown on the scrap heap strikes the Western (male?) reader as perhaps more barbarous still.[9]

But what matters most are not the facts of Danakil behavior so much as Thesiger's treatment of these facts and the origin of his information. As with Bruce's orgiastic banquet or the physical properties of Burton's Galla women, we would like to learn how he came to know what he knew. Did he observe the castrating of those who had been killed? Or, if not the actual killing, did he witness a village celebration in which the victims' genital remains were displayed and then discarded? If not, and if the trophies were not worn on the wrist, how did he discover that castration involved severing both penis and scrotum? From an informant, possibly, but as with other traditional accounts from the field, the observing eye floats free of the anthropological observer. Probably we believe Thesiger, but his shadow intervenes between ourselves as readers and the facts he reports. As the effacing of the subjective, "objectivity" opens the door to uncertainty.[10]

Once we set aside the question of how Thesiger comes by his facts, then the interest lies in their representation. On the one hand, barbaric splendors are domesticated. The Danakil, close up, are a friendly and attractive lot. On the other hand, the campaign medals of any British soldier bear witness to the savagery of European civilization. The barbaric splendor that was Thesiger's ruling passion does not differ much, he decides, from the usual way of things at home, just as Mansfield Parkyns had decided that crimping salmon and skinning eels were home-grown British cruelties. When he saw Ras Tafari's warriors marching in triumph after Sagale and the defeated generals in chains, Thesiger was too young to make the connection, but his father, for one, recognized the double edge of the spectacle: "It was the most wonderful sight I have ever seen, wild and barbaric to the last degree, and the whole thing so wonderfully staged and orderly." The wild, barbaric and thrilling triumph is also theatrically staged, "orderly." As theatrical and orderly, perhaps, as the annual celebrations of the British monarch's birthday. Or as orderly as Billy's famously rolled umbrella in his later role as the great explorer on furlough in London. On the dark side of the equation, maybe Thesiger remembered, as he wrote about the Danakil, the barbarous, homosexual and sadistic headmaster of St. Aubyns, who flogged him "with a steel shafted riding whip until I bled all over the place" and later summoned him to his office to inspect the wounds. The castrating habits of the Danakil seem no more vicious.[11]

In the years after his Danakil excursion, Thesiger was often in Ethiopia. He fought against the Italians under the command of the brilliant, very eccentric Orde Wingate, later killed in a plane crash in Burma. In 1943, after Haile Selassie had been restored to power, he asked that Thesiger be sent to Ethiopia as advisor to his son the Crown Prince, an assignment on which he spent a single frustrating year, wishing all the while that he was elsewhere and in action. When the war ended, he lived in the deserts of Arabia and with the marsh Arabs in Iraq. During summers he wandered from Persia to Pakistan and back. And in 1959 he returned again to Ethiopia. He had an audience with the emperor—"a rare distinction for an unofficial visitor"—and twice that year travelled the country with a caravan of mules. In 1966 he returned once more for celebrations of Haile Selassie's return to power, after the Italian occupation, twenty-five years before. But "the last days of a civilization," as Thesiger called them, were coming. His autobiography, *The Life of My Choice*, is dedicated "to the memory of His late Imperial Majesty Haile Selassie," and he ends his narrative with a lament: "Ethiopia, with its ancient civilization, its early Christian Church and its proud tradition of independence, is now no more than a wretched Russian satellite." The lament is equally for the emperor himself, whose long reign was a "golden age." "It is my hope," Thesiger ends, "that in time historians will assess at its true worth all he did for his country. I was privileged to have known this great man."[12]

When the Polish journalist Ryszard Kapuściński came to write *The Emperor* (1978), his account, both poignant and grotesque, of Haile Selassie's last days, he had wickedly in mind the habit, British or otherwise, of abasement before the imperial throne. One of the emperor's servants tells Kapuściński that the emperor had a dog, "a small dog, a Japanese breed," whose name was Lulu and who slept in his bed: "During various ceremonies, he would run away from the Emperor's lap and pee on dignitaries' shoes. The august gentlemen were not allowed to flinch or make the slightest gesture when they felt their feet getting wet. I had to walk among the dignitaries and wipe the urine from their shoes with a satin cloth. This was my job for ten years." In an obituary for Kapuściński, the *New York Times* sanitized the story, mentioning "the man responsible for cleaning the shoes of visiting dignitaries"—but nothing more exact. Though emperors are sometimes missing their clothes, Wilfred Thesiger, like the *New York Times,* would not be one ever to have called attention, notwithstanding his realization that the splendors of the coronation were not quite so splendid as they might have been.[13]

While it ends with a lament for passing glories, Thesiger's *The Life of My Choice* opens not only with images of imperial triumph but with homelier memories of the Addis Ababa he knew in childhood. Like a latter-day Wordsworth, he invokes a time when "[t]he earth, and every common sight,/ To me did seem/ Apparelled in celestial light,/ The glory and the freshness of a dream." Addis Ababa is full of exotic sounds, "the pitch and intonation of voices speaking Amharic," and smells, "of rancid butter, of red peppers and burning cow dung." Packs of dogs roam the streets at night, howling. "Occasional" corpses hang from gallows-trees. There are beggars missing a hand or foot, donkeys, mules, and markets where sellers offer "earthen pots, lengths of cloth, skins, cartridges, bars of salt, silver ornaments, heaps of grain, vegetables, beer." "[A]ll this," in the glory and freshness of Thesiger's dream, "combined to create a scene and atmosphere unlike any other in the world." Addis Ababa was his own lake country, the crucible in which desire was born.[14]

In 1994, at the age of 84, Thesiger returned to London and to his mother's flat in Chelsea after years of living in Kenya. He had returned to Ethiopia twice in the 1970s and then in 1996 for the hundredth anniversary of Menelik's establishing the capital in Addis Ababa. *The Life of My Choice,* he wrote, "centres on Abyssinia." So did the life that he was born into and the life he lived thereafter.[15]

❖ EVELYN WAUGH

Wilfred Thesiger detested Evelyn Waugh the moment they met at a reception during the coronation of Haile Selassie: "I disapproved of his grey suede shoes, his floppy bow tie, and the excessive width of his trousers; he struck me as flaccid and petulant and I disliked him on sight." Anyone who had seen the soft-seeming, verging-on-pudgy Waugh, with his suede shoes, bow tie and baggy trousers, in the same room with the tough, angular Thesiger might have thought they came from different planets, not from the same English stock, much less being fellow Oxonians (each with a third-class degree). Thesiger in fact underestimated Waugh, seven years his senior, who joined the Commandos in World War II and, though his life in the military was marked mostly by frustration, was not all suede shoes and bow ties. As much as Thesiger, Waugh was drawn to "distant and barbarous places." He had even aspired to go with Thesiger to the Danakil: "he asked, at second hand, if he could accompany me.... I refused." A pairing of Waugh and Thesiger would have been one of the great mismatches in the history of adventuring, a comic recasting of the famously tragic rivalry between Richard Burton and John Hanning Speke; or the less famous antagonism, in the exploration of Western Africa, between Hugh Clapperton and Dixon

Denham.[16] Perhaps Thesiger had these predecessors in mind when he imagined a less than comic outcome if he and Waugh had actually gone off together: "Had he come, I suspect only one of us would have returned."[17]

Waugh went to Ethiopia as a journalist to cover the coronation in November 1930. And cover it he did, sending home many dispatches to the London newspapers, then publishing two volumes that owed their existence to his days in Ethiopia and elsewhere in Africa: the first, a travel narrative, *Remote People* (1931); the second, that least politically correct of novels, *Black Mischief* (1932). His attitude is usually that of comic exuberance, and he found much to laugh about—but in his own way he loved the gaudy scene.

So voluminous was Waugh's reporting, and so rambunctious, that many instances might be recorded for their value as sheer entertainment. One of them comes near the end of a retrospective dispatch to the *Graphic,* published on 20 December, as "Champagne for Breakfast: A Journey to Abyssinia." In it Waugh describes a lunch he had attended at the imperial palace. It was a polite mêlée, "a large party of eighty or a hundred guests. There was no plan of the tables. The Emperor sat down at once and we wandered round and round, for a quarter of an hour or twenty minutes, hunting for our places. No one had the effrontery to look at the cards on the right and left of the Emperor so that the most honoured guests were left standing until everyone else was seated." But the food was excellent: "We had a fine luncheon of European food and wines." And then, as the meal is ending, an unscheduled amusement: "Suddenly, uninvited, a Syrian lady jumped to her feet, strode up to the Emperor and recited at great length and with lavish gestures a long complimenting ode composed by herself in Arabic, a language unintelligible to His Majesty"— as well as, no doubt, to the assembled journalists, including Evelyn

Waugh. In all, "[i]t was an odd party." This is vintage Waugh in its understated tongue-in-cheekiness and its eye for telling detail.[18]

For a journalist of Waugh's genius, the coronation was the rarest of rare opportunities, and once, on coronation day, finding himself barred from a "gebbur"—a traditional feast—for native chiefs only, he took matters into his own hands. "All right," he wrote in his voluminous diary: "will report spectacle disgusting barbarity." On 5 November, the *Times* published a dispatch from their special correspondent in Addis Ababa: "Coronation Banquet in Abyssinia, 30,000 Guests." "The Chiefs came in full dress," Waugh fibbed, "and were all armed to the teeth." And, when it came to "serious eating," the ghosts of James Bruce and other travellers stalked the banquet hall: "Large joints of raw, freshly slaughtered beef were borne down the ranks. Each man carved for himself with his own dagger. Strict etiquette was observed. The meat was raised to the mouth with the left hand, and the piece taken between the teeth was then severed by an upward slash with the dagger. Dexterity was needed to avoid amputation of the guest's nose...." On the day that he wrote this dispatch, Waugh had gone out "to see what I could barbarous gebbur" but, by 3:30, "no signs barbarity." Gullible readers back home knew what they wanted, and Waugh offered it to them with Swiftian dexterity. For all he knew, his description of the banquet may have been accurate enough.[19]

Whether in his imagination or in reality, there was plenty to keep Waugh entertained: "[I]t is to *Alice in Wonderland* that my thoughts recur in seeking some historical parallel.... How to recapture, how retail, the crazy enchantment of these Ethiopian days." During the festivities, fireworks result in "at least one nasty accident;" a cinema fails to work; some dancers sweat "so heartily that our host was able to plaster their foreheads with banknotes;" other dancers shiver from the cold "on a lawn illuminated with coloured flares;" at a race meet, "the royal enclosure was packed and the rest of the course empty of spectators." But it is Europeans who provide the very best fun: "above all, there was the great Flea Scandal and the Indiscretion about the Duke of Gloucester's Cook."[20]

The upper case lettering—"Flea Scandal" and the Duke of Gloucester's "Cook"—tells us the subject: the appetite of the press and public, akin to its appetite for "disgusting barbarity," for scandal and scandalous headlines, no matter how absurd. The local residence of the Duke of Gloucester, "like most houses in Ethiopia," was infested with fleas. The German cook asked the local servants to do something but, making no headway, complained to her English employers. "She paced up and down the room passionately, explaining her difficulties." And then, "when she turned her back it was apparent that in her agitation she had failed to fasten her skirt, which fell open and revealed underclothes of red flannel; the English party were unable to hide their amusement, and the cook, thinking that the ridicule was part of a scheme of persecution, stormed out of the house, leaving the party without their breakfast." When this piece of royal fluff, emanating from an "amiable nitwit" on the Duke's staff, hit the papers, all sorts of journalistic hell broke loose. A cable to one correspondent told him to get on the story: "*Investigate report fleas Gloucester's bed also cook red drawers left Duke breakfastless.*" The correspondent, probably Waugh himself, demurred, but by then "it was too late." The papers loved it.[21]

The great flea scandal was at most incidental to the coronation, and the object of Waugh's laughter was the press, not the emperor. But Wilfred Thesiger, for one, thought that greater solemnity was called for: "It has always seemed a pity," he wrote stodgily, "that Evelyn Waugh, the one person present with a gift for writing, was blind to the historical significance of the occasion, impercipient of this last manifestation of Abyssinia's traditional pageantry…. In *Remote People* he dwelt on 'The Great Flea Scandal', the underwear of the emperor's European housekeeper and the remarks of an American professor during the coronation service, to the exclusion of more significant observations." The American, a certain Professor W., plays a big part in Waugh's account of the proceedings, every so often whispering observations about the "Coptic ritual," then correcting himself so frequently that, it becomes obvious, he knows almost nothing about what is really going on. In his infatuation with Abyssinia's traditional pageantry, Thesiger misses the serious point of Waugh's Professor W.: that the assembled journalists and diplomats and experts at the coronation, being mostly in the dark, have to make things up on the fly. Earlier in the volume, Waugh had given a sober account of the emperor's rise to power: the chiefs "realized that there was only one man whose rank, education, intellect and ambition qualified him for the throne. This was Ras Tafari." Waugh recognized the political realities behind the grand ceremony and its odd accoutrements.[22]

We should therefore not overlook the difference between fiction and real life in face of the general outrageousness of *Black Mischief,* the kingdom of Azania, its emperor Seth—and Thesiger's assertion, in keeping with common opinion, that Waugh used his experience in Ethiopia "to parody what he had seen in *Black Mischief.*" That he used his Ethiopian experience is beyond doubt. But *Black Mischief* is not exactly a "parody." It is a burlesque. "Parody" requires a subtle and subversive nearness to its original: James Thurber's memorable take, for example, on the baroque mannerisms of the master, Henry James. *Black Mischief* is something else, and no one could call it subtle.[23]

As the story begins, Seth is preparing a proclamation: "*We, Seth, Emperor of Azania, Chief of the Chiefs of Sakuyu, Lord of Wanda and Tyrant of the Seas, Bachelor of the Arts of Oxford University, being in this the twenty-fourth year of our life, summoned by the wisdom of Almighty God and the unanimous voice of our people to the throne of our ancestors, do hereby proclaim...*" Then, looking out the window to the harbor, he sees his supporters in flight to the open sea: "'Rats,' he said; 'stinking curs. They are all running away.'" The incongruity of Seth's imperial titles and his vulgar tongue match the incongruity of Haile Selassie's exalted throne and the cook's red flannels. Bathos and burlesque overpower the pretensions of empire, but in a spirit of gaiety. By 1935, when Waugh returned to Ethiopia to report on the Italian invasion, the skies had grown much darker. In 1936, he published *Waugh in Abyssinia* (the title was not his, and he disliked the pun). Much of the volume celebrated Italy's civilizing mission in Ethiopia.[24]

In his first chapter, "The Intelligent Woman's Guide to the Ethiopian Question"—with a dubious bow to George Bernard Shaw and a gibe, possibly, at two English champions of the Ethiopian cause, Sylvia Pankhurst and Eleanor Rathbone[25]—Waugh relives the old days of the coronation when "the new Emperor was treated to every mark of independent royalty" and the international press clamored for news. But now he has a new angle of vision: the "stories of 'barbaric splendour'" demanded by distant editors produced a glut of "press messages describing the rough and often shoddy pageantry in terms that would have been barely applicable to the court of Suleiman the Magnificent or of the Mogul Emperors of India." The eccentric delights of an *Alice in Wonderland* world, as Waugh thought them earlier, now are recalled as rough and shoddy pageantry. The habits of the press seem more outlandish than entertaining. And the mind of the Emperor himself is "pathetically compounded of primitive simplicity and primitive suspicion." Everything has changed, above all Waugh's state of mind.[26]

On Waugh's behalf, he conceded the "treachery, hypocrisy and brutality" that marked the nineteenth-century partition of Africa, and he reserved some of his strongest words for Britain: "France, Germany and Belgium were the more ruthless; we the more treacherous," betraying native rulers and forever offering "louder protestations of benevolent intentions than our competitors." What's worse, "we are still preaching." But treachery, hypocrisy and brutality aside, good things came of the colonial enterprise. Administrators, "for small salaries, brought justice and order into wicked places." And for Waugh, not long since converted to Catholicism, there was above all the work of the church, of "priests and nuns, missionaries of every sect and doctors, whose whole lives were an atonement for the crimes of their countrymen." We no longer see the church's effort in so benign a light but can understand why Waugh felt as he did about the work of priests and nuns and missionaries. It is harder to understand how he came to see the Italians as bearers of new light and civilization, but that too had much to do with his new-found religion.[27]

Taxed with the question, why he became a Catholic, Waugh gave an answer in the *Daily Express* in October 1930: He was a Catholic because Catholicism is "the most complete and vital form" of Christianity, and Christianity is all that can save "western culture." In recent centuries, the educated choice has been between Christianity, on the one hand, and "a polite and highly attractive scepticism" on the other. Now it lies between "Christianity and Chaos," chaos as represented by Marxism and its "materialistic, mechanized state." Christianity is the choice, if only by default, even though Waugh concedes the attraction of Enlightenment skepticism. No longer can the western world afford the luxuries of Voltaire or Hume. A collective loss of faith is driving an "active negation of all that western culture has stood for," and "[c]ivilization … has not in itself the power of survival. It came into being through Christianity, and without it has no significance or power to command allegiance." What Waugh understands by civilization is "the whole moral and artistic organization of Europe," an ironic proposition when set against the ominous events then unfolding. All that can reasonably be said for Waugh at this point is that he simply did not realize what was coming. When Mussolini invaded Ethiopia five years after Waugh threw in his lot with Catholicism, Italy was not yet allied with Hitler, and defending the Italian mission was less obviously misguided than it seems in retrospect—or than it seemed to Rose Macaulay in 1946, looking back through the lens of war, when she called *Waugh in Abyssinia* "a Fascist tract."[28]

Lovers of Ethiopia, Waugh thought, were at best sentimentalists, "extreme lovers of the picturesque who"—this may be the most violently cringe-inducing comment in the book—"fostered lepers and eunuchs and brigand chiefs, as their milder brothers encouraged sulky yokels in England to perform folk dances on the village green." At worst, lovers of Ethiopia are those European socialists who, "in their hatred of the internal administration of Italy, nearly succeeded in precipitating world war in defence of an archaic African despotism." Looking back after the World War that in 1935 he thought had been averted, Waugh would realize how badly he had miscalled history. But he was sanguine as he watched the Italian takeover from his reporter's post in Addis Ababa. Italy and its army were not a bad European joke. During the early days of the occupation, the soldiers had endured the discomforts of the rainy season and occasional attacks by "marauding bands": "It was a severe test of morale and they stood up to it in a way which should dispel any doubts which still survive of the character of the new Italy." If the Ethiopian rains and occasional sniper fire constituted a severe test to military morale, one might be excused for lingering doubts about the new Italy. But Waugh was sure that good times lay ahead: "Plans are already being drawn up for a new city at Addis," a comment that would have annoyed Thesiger for more than one reason: he referred to the capital city only as "Addis Ababa"—the meaning in Amharic is "New Flower"—and never as "Addis." "In a few months," Waugh continues, "it will seem incredible that one drove out to dinner with a machine-gunner on the box, that one found hand-grenades on the back seat. The new régime is going to succeed."[29]

This almost delusional optimism is most conspicuous in Waugh's last chapter, "The Road." From Massawa to Asmara and across the mountains to the inland, the Italians had built an impressive new highway, planning to extend it throughout the country and then to Mogadishu in Somalia. Waugh was thrilled: "With its vast tributaries"—like the Nile—"of which Dessye is to be the point of confluence, it is at once the symbol and the supreme achievement of the Italian spirit." If this is silly, what follows is even more so: "A main road in England is a foul and destructive thing, carrying the ravages of barbarism into a civilized land—noise, smell, abominable architecture and inglorious dangers. Here in Africa it brings order and fertility." Did Waugh really suppose that a main road in Africa, however adept its engineering, would be forever immune to noise and smell and danger and, again like the Nile, bring "fertility" to the land? The building of the road and its builders inspire yet more Edenic raptures: when the workers rested, "they employed their leisure in embellishing the road they had made with little gardens of saplings and wild flowers, ornamental devices of coloured pebbles, carved eagles and wolves, fasces and heads of Mussolini." In these paradise gardens, the innocence of saplings and flowers and colored pebbles decorates and cloaks the real story: the fasces and the images of Mussolini. Waugh realized that the "eagles of ancient Rome," arriving in Ethiopia as they had come before "to our savage ancestors," may bring with them "some rubbish and some mischief," but these are of no consequence beside "the inestimable gifts of fine workmanship and clear judgment—the two determining qualities of the human spirit, by which, under God, man grows and flourishes."[30]

In *When the Going was Good* (1947), Waugh effectively renounced what he had said ten years earlier, reprinting bits and pieces of four 1930s travel narratives, including *Waugh in Abyssinia,* that comprised "all that I wish to reprint." None of the political argument survives. Waugh did not like confessing that he had been wrong and, on the one hand, said that he "found little to retract" in the opinions he had expressed; on the other hand, he conceded that some of his comments were "rather callow." He was covering up. By then he had retreated into the lush nostalgia of *Brideshead Revisited* (1945) where the lost moral organization of Europe is figured as a world of plovers' eggs, lobster, and grand summer houses. In *Brideshead,* he left Ethiopia as far behind as he possibly could.[31]

❖ SYLVIA PANKHURST

"I received weekly copies of a paper devoted to Abyssinian propaganda, edited by an English suffragette": thus Evelyn Waugh, with a sneer, in 1935. The suffragette was the indefatigable Sylvia Pankhurst, founder, publisher, and editor of the *New Times and Ethiopia News* from 1936 to 1956—"the paper for all interested in international justice" and, on later occasions, "the Anti-Fascist Weekly." Not only did the paper contain, for all its twenty years, news of Ethiopia but also of Spain, then of World War II, later of the Mau Mau uprising in Kenya and even, in June 1954, of the United States Supreme Court's verdict in *Brown v. Board of Education,* a "great" and "epoch-making" decision. Interspersed with the harder news and editorial polemics were occasional bad poetry, some of it by the editor herself, book reviews, lists of books received, and a variety of benevolent appeals. On 15 March 1941, a headline announced "Knitting for Ethiopia." The article solicited "No. 7 knitting needles in sets of four, pointed at both ends," for Miss Mary Downes and her students at Heathbrook School, who were hard at work knitting scarves and pullovers for Ethiopian soldiers. "We shall be glad to receive other offers," the editor continued, but with a caveat: "Remember no socks are required; Ethiopian warriors march bare-foot.... Sure-footed as the chamois they have defended their ancient heights these five years."[32] As a journalist Pankhurst could be schoolmarm-ish, but she was good at doing what she did. A sad postscript soon followed the appeal for knitting needles: the school was destroyed by enemy action, the students had dispersed, and Miss Downes was knitting on alone.[33]

Sylvia Pankhurst was also brave. A bold headline on 24 August 1940 read "Life of Editor Threatened." With the Battle of Britain under way and an invasion looming, Pankhurst had received two letters threatening violence. One told her to shut down the paper and that, if she did so, "no doubt sympathetic consideration will be given to you when you are tried by the Gestapo;" it also warned that if she did not stop publication, the journal "will find itself without an Editor." The other letter warned: "Do not dare go out in the dark or you will be murdered." Both letters closed with a "Heil Hitler" and one, signed by "Italian London Fascists," with a "Viva Mussolini."

Pankhurst sent the letters off to the authorities and carried on as usual.[34]

Styled by an exasperated conservative member of parliament, "*plus fuzzy-wuzzie que les fuzzy-wuzzies*," and a "horrid old harridan" by an official in the Foreign Office, Pankhurst was redoubtable, and Ethiopia became her greatest passion. Near the close of her journalistic battling, she published *Ethiopia: A Cultural History* in 1955 and dedicated it "*To His Imperial Majesty, The Emperor Haile Selassie I, Guardian of Education, Pioneer of Progress, Leader and Defender of his People in Peace and War*." The next year she settled in Ethiopia at the age of seventy-three and died four years later. Following a state funeral attended by thousands of mourners, she was buried in the grounds of Holy Trinity cathedral in Addis Ababa. Thesiger was an Ethiopian in his birth, Pankhurst by adoption, but what they shared was the sense of wonder in the presence of its splendors.[35]

Leafing through the 1,042 issues of the *New Times and Ethiopia News,* a reader may think of the Victorians, all those scholars and novelists and crusaders of huge output and urgent conviction. Born in 1882, Estelle Sylvia Pankhurst inherited both the mantle and the work habits of her suffragette mother, Emmeline. In twenty years of publishing, editing, and writing for the *New Times and Ethiopia News,* she never flagged and never missed an issue and, all the while, wrote letters of protest to newspapers and to politicians and published at least ten books on Ethiopian questions.[36] In number 1,000 of the *New Times,* 16 July 1955, when she was seventy-three, she paused to celebrate: "It was often an uphill struggle," but "'New Times and Ethiopia News' was always published whatever happened…. It is a great drama which has been unfolded week by week in those thousand issues."[37]

The *New Times,* a natural extension of Pankhurst's committed anti-Fascism, not only attacked Italy for its atrocities and harried politicians whom she regarded as guilty of appeasement but also, from its inception, defended Ethiopia against charges of barbarism that were used to justify Italy's "civilizing mission" and pointed out over and again that Ethiopia was the home of an ancient civilization and culture, the same plain truth that would become the subject of *Ethiopia: A Cultural History.* "We have been able," she wrote in the final issue of the *New Times,* "to rebut a stream of malicious representations seeking to discredit the ancient Ethiopian state."[38]

On 6 June 1936, Pankhurst published an interview with the colorful Frank Hayter, author of *In Quest of Sheba's Mines* (1935) and *The Gold of Ethiopia* (1936), who claimed to have located the mines of Solomon and the Queen of Sheba on the border between Ethiopia and the Sudan—though bad weather had so badly (but conveniently) damaged his flash apparatus that he had not been able to photograph the interior of the caves. Hayter may not have been a reliable reporter, but he was the right man to interview in the *New Times.* His Ethiopia was a happy valley. "I love the country and its people," he said, "as I do my own." There are "no cruel superstitions such as still linger on from earlier times in certain other parts of Africa." Thieves are not punished by having their hands cut off (though once they were). The country is safe: "The people are tremendously honest," and "there is no part of Abyssinia proper into which I have not gone with no more than a penknife." There are no Abyssinian brothels, as the Italians allege, though some are owned by Greeks and Armenians. Syphilis, where it exists, is the result of contact with women in the foreign brothels. And then there is slavery, a principal charge in the Italian litany of allegations and a point at issue between the emperor and the League of Nations. Hayter says: "For the talk of slavery there is only one word in my opinion, and that is 'rot'! I would prefer to be born a so-called slave in Ethiopia than a poor man in England. The relationship is patriarchal, like that of a big family." Required by the League to emancipate slaves, "the Emperor was between two fires." If they were freed, the emperor knew that "thousands of them would starve or take to brigandage, for if they had to be paid, hundreds of them would be made to do the work of a thousand." Between these fires, the emperor "told them they were free to go but need not." "If I could be born again," Hayter says, "I would be born an Abyssinian. To me it has always been a 'land of milk and honey.' I have never lacked for anything there." A happy valley, transmuted into the Israelites' promised land.[39]

The allusion to the promised land is not incidental. In the decade before the *New Times* began its crusade, an important event had taken place in Ethiopian studies: Sir Edward A. Wallis Budge, curator of Egyptian and Assyrian antiquities at the British Museum, had published a translation of the Ethiopian sacred text, the Kebra Nagast, in 1922: *The Queen of Sheba & Her Only son Menyelek; Being the History of the Departure of God & His Ark of the Covenant from Jerusalem to Ethiopia, and the Establishment of the Religion of the Hebrews & the Solomonic Line of Kings in That Country.* Budge's translation was reviewed (of course anonymously) by his colleague at the British Museum, Sir Harold Idris Bell, Keeper of Manuscripts, in the *Times Literary Supplement* for 1 June 1922. "Abyssinia," wrote Bell, "is a country which has many claims on the attention of scholars.... [I]t occupies a unque position among the countries of the Nearer East." Budge's opinion, that the Kebra Nagast is "'a very fine work,'" may "on the whole ... be accepted," though much of it "is remote from serious history." Remote from serious history or not, the Kebra Nagast struck a spark, and a second edition came out in 1932. The claim that the rulers of Ethiopia descended in a direct line from Solomon and the Queen of Sheba (also known as the Queen of the South) had a magical resonance, as did the associated claim, still an article of belief in the Ethiopian church, that the Ark of the Covenant had been taken to Ethiopia and housed in a church in Axum. This resonance was not lost on those who defended Ethiopia against Italian aggression. The features of the Abyssinian romance that now engaged the imagination were no longer raw beef and sexual license, nor the parading of savage warriors, but the ancient origins of the church and the imperial line. The new awareness of the Kebra Nagast brought the old world of Prester John back into view. That legend, Bell wrote, shows that the fascination with Abyssinia "is no recent thing."[40]

On 15 August 1936, the *New Times* published a column by Hazel M. Napier, secretary general of the "Friends of Abyssinia (Ethiopia) League of Service," with a sarcastic title: "The Benefits of Italian Rule in Ethiopia." It is a litany of Italian atrocities and Ethiopian suffering. "What of the thousands of Galla and Danakil refugees…? What of the panic-stricken women who have fled over the rough earth shielding in vain the faces of their new-born babies from the blinding gas, who have lived in terror … in the mountains, who have crouched in agony of hunger and thirst among the basalt rocks beneath a pitiless sun?" Of all these scarred and wounded, "it may be said, to quote the 'Kebra Negast,' they have suffered 'the calamity which cannot be healed.'" The casual-seeming citation of the Kebra Nagast, as though it should be equally well-known to readers as holy writ, implies the impact of Budge's translation, well-timed in the light of history, beyond the realm of antiquarian scholarship. What is more, Ethiopia is England's historical partner as a champion of the early church and in the contests of the Reformation: "What of the Ethiopian priests of the Coptic church, with their mediaeval pageantry, who have guarded the Ark of the

Covenant in this 'island of Christianity set in a sea of paganism'? These priests, who through the centuries have struggled to preserve their ancient form of Christianity from the insidious influence of Rome? Will they feel as grateful for the new benefits as the Pope of Rome?" What is happening in Ethiopia is a religious as well as a territorial war. Behind Italian aggression Hazel Napier sights an old, insidious adversary, now draped in the colors of Italian Fascism, the Pope of Rome. No doubt Evelyn Waugh was in her sights also.[41]

Only a month later, the editor of the *New Times* herself retold the ancient story from the Kebra Nagast: "The names of the Queen of Sheba and King Solomon of Judah … gain a new reality for us today from the sad martyrdom of Abyssinia. We remind ourselves; it was there the Queen of Sheba reigned. It was there she held her ancient pomp and power three thousand years ago." And, in a surprising version of Ethiopian history: "The belief of the Ethiopians in the legends of the 'Kebra Nagast' has given remarkable stability and continuity to the kingdom." Pankhurst knew that the real history of the kingdom was one of endless war and rebellion, but she accepts the grand fiction of an "ideal unity" sustaining "a royal house descended from the royal house of Judah."[42]

What inspired Pankhurst to retell the story was a volume, then recently published by Post Wheeler, the American author of *Albanian Wonder Tales* (1936), *Russian Wonder Tales* (1946), and other volumes of similar kind. Wheeler's title was lavish: *The Golden Legend of Ethiopia: The Love-Story of Mâquedâ, Virgin Queen of Axum & Shêbâ, & Solomon the Great King* (1936). Lavish as this is, it only faintly foreshadows the excess of Wheeler's prose. After a moderately sober foreword, he opens with an invocation "To The One God"—the God who designed that the Ark of the Covenant should be taken from Jerusalem, because Israel had provoked his wrath, to

Axum. To this end, *"He called Mâquedâ, Queen of this Land of AEthiopia, to Yerushaláyim, where love of her, sweet and terrible as an earthquake, leaped upon Solomon like a Nubian lion and rent the coffer of his continence,"*—I am not, as the late Molly Ivins used to delight in saying, making this up—*"and in the fulness of time it was by the son of their love ... that the Ark was brought to our holy city, Axum...."* Later, as the Queen leaves for Jerusalem, she exclaims: "I am sick of Royalty! I want a lover whose kisses shall plunder the pomegranate of my lips, a man-child whose lips shall play with the ivory haloes of my breasts." It is enough to make Karen Mercury blush, but not the editor of the *New Times*, who makes the best she can of it all, remarking that Mr. Wheeler "has drawn from all the available texts to make his book," and "has attempted to capture the atmosphere of the time." The headline introducing her commentary is: "Abyssinia's Ancient Freedom."[43]

Pankhurst's eventual cultural history of Ethiopia gathers together material appearing over the years in the *New Times* and reasonably balances the claims of clear-eyed reporting and open-eyed wonder. Her chapter on "The Glory of Aksum" provides an archaeological history of the glorious site. "The Monolithic Churches of Lalibela" celebrates "the stupendous effort," as it surely was, "of human ingenuity and skill" that went into their construction, then compares them, it seems knowledgeably, to rock-hewn churches in Egypt and India and Petra. The Kebra Nagast is "one of a large number of magnificent literary works, written in the ancient Ethiopic or Ge'ez." "A fine old book," it contains "many worthy precepts and allegories, pregnant with wise thought." But when it comes to Post Wheeler's golden legend, a note of skepticism creeps in. Wheeler makes claims, based (he says) on inscriptions, about the extent of the Queen's domains. "Great interest," Pankhurst says dryly, "would obviously attach to such inscriptions." She regrets "that Dr Post Wheeler has not published them in facsimile as an appendix to his romance." In her heart of hearts, Pankhurst probably knew that, whether the inscriptions did or did not exist, Post Wheeler was not likely to deface his romance with a scholarly appendix, however ready she was to enlist him in the great cause.[44]

In the very last issue of the *New Times,* the editor gave undiluted expression to her feelings about what was soon to be her adopted country—in a poem, hundreds of line long, vaguely resembling a Pindaric or a Miltonic ode. She called it "O Addis Ababa, O Fair New Flower." It is a story of paradise lost to Italian aggression and paradise at last regained. As poetry, it is an embarrassment. As a final emblem of Sylvia Pankhurst's romance with the golden legend of Ethiopia, it is perfect. Before the Italians came, all was harmony, a pastoral Eden before the fall:

> Gay as a springtime garden were those groves
> Graced by the crowds in fair white robes that trod
> Erect and confident, as well behoves
> The people of a land beloved of God.
> And songs rose gaily 'mid those happy folk
> Who never yet had borne an alien yoke.

"Studious" schoolboys and "lithe-limbed" schoolgirls play their customary roles. And, as if on some medieval tapestry,

> ... here a noble lady rides to town,
> Sedately garbed, but jauntily astride;
> Her pony gay caparisoned, her state
> Denoted by those runners at her side
> Who move so gracefully at such a rate.

But then the Italians arrive:

> Baleful the stench of burning fills the air,
> The heart-sick odour of our martyred flesh,
> And horrid fears the trembling thoughts enmesh;
> Hot-foot the rumour speeds: "They're eating men!"

And:

> Fond husbands roped to their domestic trees,
> Powerless to aid, must see with frantic eyes
> Their dear wives scourged by ruthless Blackshirt bands.

Until, finally, pastoral order is restored:

> These Eucalyptus, lovely as of yore,
> Shall sway their leafy bows with every breeze.

The emperor reclaims the throne:

> And every eye in that rejoicing throng
> Turned oft to him, as though some loftier power
> Guided his judgment, ever true and strong.

And all thoughts are with the heroes who have been lost. Life is consecrated now "to one high aim," "To Cherish thee, Ethiopia. Motherland."[45]

Uncommonly bad though the poetry is, this ode to Addis Ababa lays open the sources behind Pankhurst's vision: the "golden haze" through which she viewed Ethiopia and its cause equally marked a long tradition in English verse and art. The haze was golden not just because the mines of Solomon lay in Ethiopia or because Solomon began the imperial line, but because Spencer, Milton, Pope, Johnson, Grey, Wordsworth, Coleridge, Gainsborough, Constable, Turner, and William Morris had all in one way and another painted the scene, in words and on canvas. In Pankhurst's poetic hands, the often stark landscape of Ethiopia becomes a green and pleasant motherland (in contrast to the Fascist fatherland), another earthly paradise of "springtime" gardens, "tender verdure," and "sun-splashed shade," home to wandering minstrels and young lovers, a "fair radiant scene." In a lyric for May in William Morris's *The Earthly Paradise* (1868–70)—his very long (some would say endless) poem in which a band of medieval wanderers seek a land of everlasting life—the Lord of Love passes by and "takes possession of his flowery throne,/ Ringed round with maids, and youths, and minstrelsy." Pankhurst did not need any single source for her Ethiopian minstrels and lovers, but she began life as an artist, and Morris had visited her family home when she was a child. Her ideal Ethiopia is a pre-Raphaelite world.[46]

CHAPTER FOUR

"I'm Going to Ethiopia": Recent Visitors

Wₕₕₐₗₑ ₛₕₑ ₐₛ ₐₒᵣₖᵢₙₑ ᵣₐₙ *I Didn't Do It for You: How the World Betrayed a Small African Nation* (2005), an account of Eritrea's role as a pawn in chess games of the great powers; as Ethiopia's unhappy dependent post-1952; and as her not always happy neighbor post-1993, Michela Wrong found herself conversing with a Pakistani businessman in the Cairo airport. He asks what she does. "I'm a journalist," she says, "I'm writing a book about Eritrea. That's where I'm going now." What follows is comic but also calculated, perhaps invented in part or even in sum, but not the less engaging:

His brow furrowed, he must have misheard. 'You are writing a book about Algeria?'

'No, not Algeria. Eritrea.'

'Nigeria?' He was floundering now.

'No.'

A wild guess. 'Al-Jazeera?'

'No, no. *Eritrea.*' Enunciating the word with the exaggerated lip movements of a teacher addressing a class with special needs, I searched for some explanatory shorthand. 'You know. Small country on the Red Sea. Used to be part of Ethiopia. It's only two hours' flight from here. I'm waiting for my connection.' There was a brief silence. This seasoned traveller looked both flummoxed and embarrassed. 'I'm sorry. But I've simply never heard of the place.'

This is what the travel-writing traveller dreams of, a destination not known to others. If a "seasoned" traveller like Wrong's soap powder salesman doesn't know anything about Eritrea, all the better. When Wrong tells others her subject, "the reaction would be a sympathetic nod and ruminative silence as the other person tried to work out whether I was talking about a no-frills airline, a Victorian woman novelist or, perhaps, some obscure strain of equine disease." At this point, some of the comedy is surely manufactured. Did anyone ever suppose that Eritrea was an airline or a Victorian novelist or an equine disease? Unlikely, but it gets the story going and heightens the lure of what is now to come.[1]

The unknown calls us. Stuart Munro-Hay's named his well-crafted cultural and historical guide, *Ethiopia, the Unknown Land* (2002). Perhaps the publishers insisted. There cannot be many lands, certainly not in Africa, that have had so much European attention as Ethiopia—as John Camden Hotten realized many years ago. When I began this project, I had no idea how large was the roster of post-war visitors. Excluding learned studies like Munro-Hay's, Donald Levine's *Wax and Gold* (1965) and his *Greater Ethiopia* (1974), or Richard Pankhurst's *The Ethiopians: A History* (1998), I count at least twenty-five volumes that qualify in a general way as narratives of travel. The list that follows is chronological. With the titles in view, it will be easier to gauge the contours of the territory.

—David Roden Buxton, *Travels in Ethiopia* (1949).

—Lionel Ferguson, *Into the Blue: the Lake Tana Expedition, 1953* (1955).

—Douglas L. Busk, *The Fountain of the Sun: Unfinished Journeys in Ethiopia and the Ruwenzori* (1957).

—Edna S. Heffner, *Ethiopia: Land beyond the Rift* (1957).

—Herbert M. Hanson and Della Hanson, *For God and Emperor* (1958).

—Thomas Pakenham, *The Mountains of Rasselas: An Ethiopian Adventure* (1959).

—Barbara Toy, *In Search of Sheba: Across the Sahara to Ethiopia* (1961).

—Dervla Murphy, *In Ethiopia with a Mule* (1968).

—Len Shaw, *Into the Hidden Land* (1970).

—Duncan Forbes, *The Heart of Ethiopia* (1972).

—Thelma Tonkin, *Ethiopia, with Love* (1972).

—Alan Caillou, *Sheba Slept Here* (1973).

—Melvin Bolton, *Ethiopian Wildlands* (1976).

—Paul B. Henze, *Ethiopian Journeys: Travels in Ethiopia, 1969–72* (1977).

—Charlie Pye-Smith, *The Other Nile* (1986).

—Leslie Woodhead, *A Box Full of Spirits: Adventures of a Film-Maker in Africa* (1987).

—Edward Ullendorff, *The Two Zions: Reminiscences of Jerusalem and Ethiopia* (1988).

—Philip Marsden-Smedley, *A Far Country: Travels in Ethiopia* (1990).

—Kay Kaufman Shelemay, *A Song of Longing: An Ethiopian Journey* (1991).

—Kevin Rushby, *Eating the Flowers of Paradise: A Journey through the Drug Fields of Ethiopia and Yemen* (1998).

—Julia Stewart, *Eccentric Graces: Eritrea & Ethiopia Through the Eyes of a Traveler* (1999).

—Virginia Morell, *Blue Nile: Ethiopia's River of Magic and Mystery* (2001).

—Tahir Shah, *In Search of King Solomon's Mines* (2002).

—Mimi LaFollette Summerskill, *In the Land of Solomon and Sheba* (2002).

—Philip Marsden, *The Chains of Heaven: An Ethiopian Romance* (2005).

—Michela Wrong, *I Didn't Do it for You: How the World Betrayed a Small African Nation* (2005).

In 1957, Northrop Frye published the taxonomic *tour de force* that he called *Anatomy of Criticism*. It was a gospel text at the time and remains a cornerstone in the tradition of literary-critical formalism. Its discriminations among categories of literature—comedy, romance, tragedy, and irony—that are "broader than, or logically prior to" any particular genres provide a point of entry here, for this is another juncture where the story of Ethiopian travel writing merges with that of travel writing in general. Travel writing as such finds no place in Frye but self-evidently falls under what he calls "the mythos of summer," which is the mythos of romance: "The essential element of plot in romance is adventure." Philip Marsden's subtitle to *The Chains of Heaven*, an "Ethiopian Romance," would do as well for many (though not every one) of these narratives.[2]

Their titles suggest something of their range, in all combinations of memoir, adventure, quest, and longing.[3] They also illustrate something of what has happened to book titles since the days of James Bruce, when they were more straightforward: *Travels to Discover the Source of the Nile, in the Years 1768, 1769, 1770, 1771, 1772 and 1773*. Or Mansfield Parkyns's: *Life in Abyssinia*. Or even Burton's *First Footsteps in East Africa*, self-promoting in its overstatement of the facts but still far from our own higher-flying ways. Straightforward description is now the exception (*Travels in Ethiopia; Ethiopian Journeys*) and metaphorical enticement more common (*A Song of Longing; Eccentric Graces*). One way and another, golden legends abound.

Whatever the title, however, the quest theme is seldom absent and is very often to the fore, but nowadays seldom involves a simple tale of triumph. Whereas Bruce gloried in reaching the Blue Nile and Burton in surviving Harar, now the quest is more likely to be ambiguous; the seeker, more often frustrated, doubtfully successful, or arriving at an unexpected destination. In Frye's taxonomy, the "complete form of romance is clearly the successful quest." Yet successful quests, like Bruce's or Burton's, can bring on fits of melancholy while less successful quests and flawed romances can be oddly satisfying. Certainly they better suit the needs of the modern, now that the "unknown" is likely to be more fiction than fact.[4]

❖ IRONICAL ROMANCE: FERGUSON, PAKENHAM, SHAH

In 1953, two Cambridge undergraduates pondered, on a cold English night, the long vacation ahead. Lionel Ferguson asks his friend John Esplen: "What will you do?" The answer: "Anything, except stay here in England for four months." Perhaps Algeria? Well, no, "Everybody goes to Algeria." They get out an atlas. "We turned to Africa, and soon spotted a blue blob in the middle of north-eastern Africa. Into the blue, we thought. It was a lake ... Lake Tana.... Source of the Blue Nile. The Lake Tana Expedition was born." "[R]elatively unexplored, practically unknown source of the most mysterious river in the world—the Blue Nile," Lake Tana is as fair a destination as can be found, now that "relatively" unexplored and "practically" unknown locations are as much as can be hoped for.

What the expedition turns into is a travelling entertainment for five undergraduates in a van-like, much-used Ford V8, purchased for £95, christened "Winnie," and fixed up with new engine, new tires, a new paint job of "cool pastel green," and inscribed on each of the front doors, "Lake Tana Expedition 1953." Along the way, at Benghazi on the Libyan coast, an Arabic inscription is added to the doors, announcing that this is a "Geography Kindergarten party going to Africa." It should have read: "Student Geographical Expedition to Ethiopia."[5]

The student-adventurers often do but sometimes do not seem quite to realize their quixotic look. An early, throwaway "and all that" signals undergraduate insouciance: "John ... thought of Ethiopia as one of the wonders of the world—Prester John, the Queen of Sheba, Solomon, and all that." But, self-deprecating fun notwithstanding, the resulting volume is equipped with the apparatus of sober adventuring: the usual map of the journey on the endpapers (Dover to Gibraltar, across North Africa to Ethiopia, then home by way of Damascus, Ankara and points east); a list of supplies such as nineteenth-century explorers often included in their narratives (sleeping bags, 24 rolls of toilet paper, a packet of safety pins, iodine, morphine, Epsom salts, etc., etc., and, for the Ford, any number of replacement parts); some pious and rather murky reflections ("I would also like to make it clear that an expedition, even by undergraduates, must always be specific in purpose. This makes it necessary to fulfil many obligations that are embodied in it"); and even a foreword by the distinguished General Sir Brian Robertson, Bt., G.C.B., K.C.M.G., D.S.O., M.C., later first Baron Robertson of Oakbridge: "To congratulate the members of the expedition is proper and I do it with pleasure. But I also congratulate the University of Cambridge for arranging her affairs in such a way that her undergraduates are encouraged to make expeditions of this kind. To travel is always good, but to travel far and hard on little money and in limited time is first-class education." General Sir Brian no doubt recognized his puffery for what it was, but he does his best: Ethiopia "is richly endowed by nature, and has, for the most part, an excellent climate, but it is certainly not easily accessible." "Not easily accessible" adds up to a passably modest endorsement of the Lake Tana expedition and its distant, if not all that distant, goal.[6]

The travellers finally arrive at the lake, after two months on the road and a boat trip from Suez to Massawa, and find themselves living not in the rough conditions they had expected but in a reasonably well-appointed villa, the result of some good connections. And the lake, also contrary to their hopes, is "rather disappointing," its waters "muddy" and its surface "ruffled." The Lake Tana Expedition is in danger of petering out into inconsequence, if not outright disenchantment. Yet everything turns out for the best, even if the best is not what the travellers could have anticipated.[7]

On a boat trip around the lake, they watch the sun go down, "conjuring all the brilliance, the mystery and magic of an African night behind the low silhouette of Dek," an island near their anchorage. This at least catches up with their expectations: "It was the Africa we had dreamed about as schoolboys." But the moment of recognition, Aristotle's *anagnorisis*, is reserved for something other than the customary splendors of an African sunset. The next day, in the ancient monastery of St. Stephen on the island of Dek, the chief priest shows them around, then takes them to a second building with "an inner chamber, dark and vault-like." This Gothic chamber, not the lake itself nor even the sunset, is the destination they had not known they were seeking: "There, lying on trestles and covered with richly embroidered cloths of green, pink, red, gold and silver, were three coffins." In the candle light, the mingled colors of the embroidered cloths mimic the spectacle of the African sun going down. The priest draws the covers off each coffin in turn to reveal, in the flickering light, the preserved remains of three Ethiopian kings. "It was a weird sight." The young men, not much more than boys, really, have smelled mortality: "the stench was powerful." But they look closely. King Fasilides's toenails are colored red with henna. Zara Yacob's sword is by his side. The joyful, mock-heroical undergraduate lark has come to an unexpected climax. But what "a marvelous ending." Boyish enthusiasm mixes with intimations of mortality, and the travellers head happily home. Lionel Ferguson is not the most sophisticated of writers, but his chronicle of the Lake Tana Expedition, with its Hardy boys' adventuring sealed by the imprimatur of General Robertson and its high-spirits in the presence of decaying monarchs, offers fair helpings of tongue-in-cheek mixed with recollections of more confident times: a "geography kindergarten party going to Africa," on the one hand; a "student geographical expedition to Ethiopia," on the other.[8]

Thomas Pakenham, later in his life the author of the magisterial *The Scramble for Africa* (1991), is a more sophisticated writer than Ferguson and has a special knack for converting a failed quest into successful adventure. Like *Into the Blue, The Mountains of Rasselas* begins as an undergraduate frolic, an overture of sorts to *The Scramble for Africa*. In a "Venetian Gothic house overlooking the Thames at Oxford" conversation turns "to talk of amusing places where we might spend the summer holidays after Schools." Abyssinia is high on the list: "was this not the land of Prester John and the Queen of Sheba" and "the birthplace of *Black Mischief* and *Scoop?*" Was it not, that is, home both to golden legends and to the impish irreverence of Evelyn Waugh, who happened to be a family friend? A perfect combination. At first, however, the trip seems too expensive, but then a Dominican friend comes up with a destination and a quest. There is a "Mountain near Gondar," he tells Pakenham, "called Wachni"—or Wehni, in a more common spelling. The upper case "M" in "Mountain," like the upper-case "E'" in Ferguson's "Expedition," announces the quest. The princes of the blood were confined on Wehni: "Johnson describes the customs in *Rasselas*," Pakenham's Dominican friend tells him, and "the extraordinary thing is, my dear Thos, that no European's ever set eyes on Wachni...." The lure of being first is as usual irresistible: after "diligent research"—a prerequisite, of course—Pakenham concludes that the magic mountain is indeed "unvisited by any European" and decides that the quest promises to "add something"—he concedes that it is not clear "exactly what"—to historical knowledge. It is all "spiced by the romantic associations of *Rasselas*." Fact and legend commingle. But the quest itself runs into one frustration after another. It is a satisfying outcome.[9]

When he locates the mountain, some eighty miles east of Gondar, Pakenham is unprepared for what he has found: not a mountain in the ordinary sense but an outcropping of rock known as an amba, hundreds of feet high in the shape of a thumb. He sees buildings on the summit, but a landslide has blocked the only path, steps cut into rock up the sheer mountain face, and his ascent comes to an ignominious end: under overhanging rock, he tries to crawl around the landslide and wedges himself into an impossible position. He sees his guides, skeptical from the first about the whole idea, grinning at his plight: "I wondered humbly what would happen to me." An agile "goat-like man" who has led the ascent rescues him, "flying up the rock face" until, a few feet from the hapless victim, "he took a sickle-shaped knife, that rested in his frizzy hair like a pencil over an errand-boy's ear, and stretched its handle to me. I seized it gratefully. Soon I was restored to the ground."[10]

After this embarrassment, Pakenham borrows a climbing rope "from a gym mistress at the British Embassy" and, undaunted, sets out again, this time in the company of a German doctor from the World Health Organization and an Ethiopian medical student as their interpreter. But their local guides are unreliable. Travelling by a different route than before, they keep getting lost. They find themselves stranded and have to send a messenger for help. Finally a rescue party arrives, among them the provincial governor, who gives a "short speech of welcome." And then comes a moment of recognition, as at the monastery of St. Stephen in *Into the Blue,* when the quest is wonderfully recast. Pakenham attempts a reply but is interrupted by a young boy who shyly "offered first me, and then Dr Jäger a small posy of Alpine flowers, marigolds and crocuses, and a spray of wild thyme and rosemary." Like the sanctuary of the three dead kings, this is the destination the traveller could not have anticipated but that turns out to hold the journey's meaning. "This entirely unmanned me. We had blundered like schoolboys into his private paradise," gotten stranded, had to be rescued, "and this was our reward—not recriminations but flowers culled from the Happy Valley. (No other valley, I well knew, could have yielded such fertile treasure)." It is a moment "more moving, I think in retrospect, than any in all the months of my wandering." Johnson's fantasy valley takes on the reality of marigolds and crocuses, thyme and rosemary. Rosemary being for remembrance, Pakenham keeps the flowers, now "lying dusty" in his cupboard, "like bones in an ossuary" (or like the bodies of Fasilides and Zara Yacob). "I can hardly look upon them with equanimity. They have become the symbol for me of my love affair with the Mountain." Irony thrives on what could not have been foretold, the deflection of quest, here, into the realm of happenstance. The flowers are like an old love-letter, still able "to make my heart leap with pain and joy to remember the green table-land of Belesa, the valley and the Mountain."[11]

After the failure of this second attempt, Pakenham consoles himself with an ascent of Amba Geshen, another of the fortresses where the Abyssinian princes were said to have been shut away. He believes it is the site of Milton's earthly paradise, "a Rock/ Of Alabaster piled up to the Clouds:" "At the seven hundred and third step—I could not resist counting them—we reached the doorway which in Milton's verses would have held the Gates of Paradise." But this paradise is nothing to write home about. It lies behind iron gates and barbed wire, an unromantic medley of huts for monastic buildings, peopled by an occasional monk and "even a few withered nuns." The view from the summit is not of a green and happy valley, like that from Wehni, but a "stupendous, melancholy void." The mountain of Wehni becomes by contrast an ever more desirable goal. The stage is set for one last disappointment.[12]

Pakenham plans a third attempt on the Mountain, this time by helicopter, a less romantic alternative to an ascent from the ground but better than nothing at all. Even this plan, however, comes to naught. As if by destiny, the helicopter self-destructs—"the rotor had apparently been assembled upside down"—and the vision of standing on the summit of Wehni melts into air. Yet all is not absolutely lost. On a flight by private plane from Gondar to Addis Ababa, the pilot, an American, asks Pakenham if he would like to fly over the Mountain "in a real aeroplane." And they do: "The plane swept on across the tableland a mere 500 feet above it. The Happy Valley at last, and the Mountain." At the awesome sight of the Mountain, the pilot breaks into American patois: "Do you really mean people were stuck on the top? ... Boy, what a goddam place to spend your life!"[13]

Back in England, when Pakenham returns, everything is grey: the apartment buildings, the grass, his long-postponed office job. Improbable rumors are flying about—or perhaps they are his own authorial inventions, dreams of what-might-have-been. Is it true that he "found princes still living on the Mountain fettered with chains of solid gold"—a twist on the golden legend? Or that he married "an Ethiopian princess"? Even if these are self-created fantasies of ironic grandeur, one detail rings true: "Somebody even asked me if I thought King Zog," the Albanian ruler with the engaging name, "was secure on his throne." With that, "I began to try to forget about Ethiopia."[14]

But a final act of homage remains. In the seventeenth century an Ethiopian named Zagachrist turned up in Paris, claiming to be the rightful heir to the Solomonic line, an Ethiopian equivalent of the Mohawk Kings who came to London in the next century; or of Omai, the Pacific islander who returned to England with Captain Cook and enchanted the natives, Fanny Burney among them. Zagachrist made quite a splash at Versailles; the court ladies were very fond of him. But the European climate was too hard, and he died after only six years. Pakenham finds his grave outside of Paris, another reminder of the dead kings at St. Stephen's. Zagachrist's epitaph is also a perfect epitaph to *The Mountains of Rasselas*: "Ci gist, le roi d'Ethiopie,/ L'original ou la copie./ Le fut-il? ne le fut-il pas?/ La mort a fini les debats." The ironic see-saw that Pakenham rides so well comes to rest in death, which puts an end to debate.[15]

As adventurers, Ferguson and Pakenham are amateurs who make the most of their amateur standing. Tahir Shah is a professional who masquerades capably as an amateur when it serves him, as it does when he cranks up his narrative at the beginning of a story.

Like his earlier *Trail of Feathers* (2001), an account of a search for the "birdmen of Peru," *In Search of King Solomon's Mines* begins as if by accident, in a tourist trap in Jerusalem. Shah's quests are unrealistic from their start, but they turn out to be grounded in a certain odd reality. In *Trail of Feathers,* a chance meeting with "an elderly French-man" at an auction of shrunken heads in London sets him searching for the birdmen of the Peruvian jungle—where he discovers the hallucinogenic properties of ayahuasca. *In Search of King Solomon's Mines,* like *Treasure Island,* begins with a map, but it is a palpable fake. Browsing in the Old City, Shah finds himself at "Ali Baba's Tourist Emporium" where he sees "an inky hand-drawn map hung on the back wall." It depicts an exotic landscape with a trail ending in "an oversized 'X'." Ali Baba, "an old dog of a man" with a pot belly hinting at "a diet rich in fat-tailed sheep," tells him the map is not for sale. "But is it a treasure map?" Shah asks. Well, of course. And "where's the treasure supposed to be?" It is a map of King Solomon's mines—for sale, of course, at the right price. Shah buys it and, at Ali Baba's the next day, sees on the wall another "inky hand-drawn map." "[T]his is fraud," he fumes. But Ali Baba has the answer for him: "The map I sold you was the real one…. I'm giving you a head start in your search." Shah is a skilled fabulist, and there is no need to care whether Ali Baba's Tourist Emporium, or Ali Baba, or the maps, ever existed at all. They are the ivory gate of false dreams through which Virgil, and now Tahir Shah, emerge from the underworld, Virgil to found Rome, Shah to go looking for the fabled mines.[16]

The next time we see him, he is in Addis Ababa, this time with a real map in his hands. We learn that his father and grandfather had also searched for Solomon's mines. His father, as Shah tells the story, had begun with a big map of the Middle East on which, "taking a handful of stones," he "had placed them on key points": Petra, Mecca, Damascus, and others. On his map of Ethiopia Shah does the same, marking with pebbles (that he finds conveniently in his pocket) places where there may be gold: the Afar, "where testicle-hunters once roamed;" Harar, where the hyenas are the guardians of gold; the ancient monastery of Debra Damo, near Axum; Lalibela; Gondar; a remote location near the southern border, home to Ethiopia's only legal gold mine; and, due west of Addis Ababa near the border with Sudan, the unnamed place where Herodotus said that gold was abundant. Shah has boxed the compass: Gondar, Lalibela, and Addis Ababa at (roughly) the center; Afar and Harar to the east; Axum to the north; a gold mine to the south; and the mysterious gold of Herodotus to the western frontier, where dreams end.[17]

E. M. Forster defined a "story" as moving from "and then" to "and then;" a plot, as depending on interior connections and causes. Travel narratives need a plot if they are not to be one "and then" after another. Shah's seven pebbles are his story; his plot is gold. King Solomon's mines, like Ali Baba's map, in fact have rather little to do with it. But the search gives narrative concentration, or the suggestion of it, to this wide-ranging look at all the corners of the Ethiopian scene, north, south, east, and west, complete with monks and monasteries, whores and brothels, bandits, broken-down vehicles and car wrecks, recalcitrant mules, gold mines both legal and illegal, even the occasional murder. Shah has married the kind of quest that follows a single theme along a narrative road to another kind that seeks a far-away goal, to be reached at the end of a long journey.

The actual story behind Shah's quest seems to have gone something like this. From his introduction we learn that Wilfred Thesiger first suggested Ethiopia. And then, perhaps, looking for a new adventure after his flying trip to Peru, Shah comes across the writings of the eccentric Englishman Frank Hayter who searched in the 1930s for Ethiopian gold, mined the search for two books, and provided Sylvia Pankhurst with some good copy for her *New Times*. Undoubtedly Shah knew about Hayter before he began his journey—"By the time we reached Addis Ababa I was determined to find out more about Frank Hayter"—though we only hear of him in Addis Ababa when Shah reads *The Gold of Ethiopia* (1936): "With such a title it had seemed an obvious book to buy." Before we hear of Hayter in the narrative, Shah has set the pebbles down on his map—and credited Herodotus with the one that he places on a vaguely specified location to the west. But it was Hayter who claimed to have found Solomon's mines on a western mountain called Tullu Wallel, more or less exactly where Shah puts his pebble. Hayter's account is likelier by far than Herodotus or Ali Baba's map to have provided Shah his entry point. Tullu Wallel is his destination from the start, but in the windings of the narrative, he gathers up the other pebbles as he goes along. Tullu Wallel, however, will be his impossible Mountain.[18]

As he finally nears his goal, a drunken, syphilitic old man tells him that Tullu Wallel is haunted: "The Devil lives on the mountain." And: "He'll kill you and eat your brains." Devil or no devil, Shah and his companion Samson, a former gold miner and taxi diver turned guide, hire a string of mules and muleteers and press on. They tell villagers that they are missionaries who will rid them of the devil. Missionaries, it's said, have been to the mountain before "but never came down." The mountain curses anyone who climbs it. But they start to climb. After hours in heavy rain they find a cave entrance such as Hayter had described: "We had found it. We had found the entrance to Solomon's mines." With their torches, they enter the cave, swarming with bats. They move forward in the darkness, and then: "after twenty feet, we hit a rock wall and the cave came to an abrupt end. With the bats still swooping and diving around us, we searched for a passageway or a brick wall or a door. But there was no way forward." It is the deadest of dead ends.[19]

Seven months later, Shah returns to Ethiopia and mounts another expedition to Tullu Wallel with even worse results than before. As they approach the mountain, rain comes down in sheets and turns to hail. Food and drinking water run out. The mules are out of control. Everyone is sick. Shah has fallen into a nest of soldier ants: "[b]eing eaten alive by soldier ants is incredibly painful;" the quest for the mines is "destroying not only me but those with me." It is the end of the story, the commander orders a retreat, and they all head back to the main road: "Frank Hayter's secret was still safe, as was the exact whereabouts of King Solomon's mines."[20]

Earlier Shah wonders why Hayter published no photograph of the cave although E. J. Bartleet, his friend and fellow-explorer (who had not himself gone to Tullu Wallel), retold the tale, publishing a small, blurry snapshot with a caption, "*The entrance to the Queen of Sheba's caves.*" Perhaps, Shah says, Hayter "feared it would help others identify the place." He hardly need have worried: the photograph that Bartleet published could have come from almost anywhere. But Shah has started a hare. His own volume includes several handsome illustrations: of his companion Samson reading a Bible; of the illegal gold mine at Bedakaysa, a scene that could come from Sebastião Salgado; of the monastery at Debra Damo; of Frank Hayter, smoking a cigarette, standing before a huge leopard skin, and wearing pith helmet, shorts, and laced-up leather boots; of Shah himself, looking like a smiling Puck in protective gear, holding three heavy bars of Ethiopian gold; and various other images of the Ethiopian scene. But there is no photograph of Tullu Wallel, or of its cave, or of the mules and muleteers who helped Shah on his way to the mountain. Tullu Wallel has disappeared amid rain and hail. Tahir Shah's secret, like Hayter's, remains perfectly safe.[21]

❖ PILGRIMS: RUSHBY, MARSDEN

While the quest theme is now often inflected with irony, the idea of pilgrimage remains immune to the deprecations of self-constructed failure. Quests manage well enough without doses of the spiritual. The undergraduates setting out for Lake Tana are not pilgrims, even though they eventually find themselves at a shrine of Ethiopian kings. A pilgrimage without the spiritual, however, is a self-contradiction. And, while it is a normal aim of quest to find something (the source of the Nile) or do something (climb Mount Wehni) that nobody, or no man, or no woman, or no European has done before, pilgrimage depends on acts of reiteration. Millions of Muslims travel to Mecca each year for the hajj, the occasion of Burton's *Pilgrimage to Al-Medinah and Meccah* (1855, 1856), a quest that he disguised in the robes of pilgrimage. The reiterations of pilgrimage take forms both sacred and secular: following the footsteps of Samuel Johnson in the Hebrides, for example; visiting the grave of a particular hero, perhaps Richard Burton's marble tent, at the church of St. Mary Magdalene, Mortlake; or revisiting one's own past, ancestral or private. These journeys reenact what has happened before, whether in one's own life or others'. Pilgrimage is a private affair; quest is public. Kevin Rushby's *Eating the Flowers of Paradise* and Philip Marsden's *The Chains of Heaven* each take part in the ritual of pilgrimage, each announcing the claims of paradise and of heaven.

The "flowers of paradise" in Rushby's story are the psychoactive leaves of the qat tree, *catha edulis,* the same narcotic about whose varieties Burton fancied himself expert. The drug, a cultural staple of life in the Ethiopian south and especially in Yemen, is banned in the United States but not in Britain, leading perhaps to a bibliographic anomaly. Published in Britain in 1998, *Eating the Flowers of Paradise* was subtitled *A Journey through the Drug Fields of Ethiopia and Yemen.* Published a year later in the United States, the dust jacket (though not the title page) sanitizes the subtitle: *One Man's Journey through Ethiopia and Yemen.* Perhaps the publishers feared that the original would inhibit sales in Kansas. Rushby's journey takes him from Addis Ababa to Harar, then through Djibouti, across the Gulf of Aden to Yemen, and finally to San'a, the ancient highland capital of Yemen. It is a journey of perhaps a thousand miles. Among his guide stars are Richard Burton, Arthur Rimbaud—and his own younger self.

The narrative opens with longings for paradise lost. Rushby is in Malaysia, remembering earlier days in Yemen: "I knew all along, despite the passing years and even one false dawn when my return was abruptly cut short by Yemen's civil war, I knew that I would have to return and see if those pearl strings [of memory] were anything more than piles of dusty discarded leaves and memories polished by time—the Lotos-land would have to be revisited, the paradise regained." Other of Rushby's books are *Hunting Pirate Heaven* (2003), about pirate haunts in the *Indian Ocean; Chasing the Mountain of Light* (1999), about the Koh-i-Noor diamond; and, most recent, *Paradise: A History of the Idea that Rules the World* (2007). Paradise is his ruling passion.[22]

He knows that he is playing the passionate pilgrim on his way to San'a. Why not, after all, fly straight to Yemen? A travel agent tells him that it would be quicker and cheaper. But it would be too easy. He tells the agent, "I need to approach things a little more slowly."

And even the agent agrees, "You may be right." In Harar, his Arab companion asks him, "When you want to reach something but must do a hard and difficult journey first, that is like a Muslim hajj, isn't it?" Rushby nods, "It could be." "What do you call it in English?" "A pilgrimage." It would be presuming too much to say that it is like the hajj. But it could be.[23]

Of course any pilgrim intending to convert the experience of pilgrimage into a book is also engaged in a quest: the book is the quarry. Habits of the private pilgrimage intersect with habits of the public quest, and sometimes the pilgrim may look like his adventuring counterpart. When Rushby arrives in Yemen, he hears about the nearby Sultanate of Yafa, "a large province of 8,000-foot mountains and deep valleys," a Yemenite equivalent of the Ethiopian highlands. "You must not go to Yafa," he is told. "It is too far and its people are not good." Yafa is dangerous. And mysterious: "I began to ask everyone I met about Yafa but most were equally vague." One man says: "They are Jews"; another, "they make trouble." In 1953 the British governor of Aden called the area "uncivilized and turbulent in the extreme." With such auspicious signals, "I resolved to go there immediately." Yafa is a pilgrim's detour into adventure, justified in the event by the discovery that qat, in Yafa, is high grade.[24]

Yafa also provides Rushby with an unlikely, and somewhat dubious, first. In a taxi from Aden he finds himself travelling with a cheerful Russian surgeon who practices at a hospital in Yafa and whose main business is patching up victims of local violence: "Once a shop in the souk exploded and we had ten people for amputation. One man was almost dead, we amputated both legs and seven days later he went home. These people are very tough, really." When they arrive in Yafa, Rushby hears "the urgent stuttering of a distant machine gun," and his friend Sergei sighs: "More work for me! Ah,

Kevin. Welcome to Yafa—you are our first tourist." Being the first tourist is a faint approximation of the distinction that every explorer seeks but a first nonetheless.[25]

Rushby also works a final change on the motif of the unfulfilled quest. As his journey nears its end in San'a—"there could be no better place to find the perfect qat session than in San'a"—he dreams of a session "in the palace of the last king of Yemen." He expects his friend Hassan, descended from kings, to make the arrangements, and fancy takes over. There will be "a grand room with ornate stucco arabesques above the windows, aqds"—demi-lune windows—"of exquisite artfulness, some old pipes once smoked by the Imam, opulent acres of cushions." A lutanist will sing. The qat will be highest grade. And Hassan will be there "representing his illustrious ancestor by whose grace we had those leaves in our hands." They set out in Hassan's estate car and, when the palace comes into view, Hassan stops. "See it!" he says, "I promised you would chew at the Rock Palace." At the Rock Palace, that is, but not in it because Hassan's relative, said to have the keys, is unluckily in prison. Hassan gets out of the car, opens the rear door and climbs in. Rushby and his English friend Tim climb over their seats to join him. Rushby laughs. "Why are you laughing?" Tim asks. The obvious answer: "I wanted to take qat in paradise—the most beautiful place in Yemen—and we're in Hassan's car boot." Well, says Tim, "don't you know what they say, 'If your heart is at peace'"—and here the pilgrim resumes his mantle—"'even a donkey's arsehole can be a mafraj.'" A mafraj is "a restful room for taking qat," be it the boot of a car or a donkey's arse. The unrealized quest has been an illusion; the real trick "is to know when you're happy." The pilgrim seeks happiness best in himself, not in hunting down happy valleys or steep ambas or rock palaces.[26]

As the story ends, Rushby, Tim, and Hassan, in their qat-induced reveries, contemplate the meaning of it all. Across the valley from them on a mountainside are caves housing ancient tombs. Hassan tells the story of a man who, dreaming of riches, writes on pieces of paper "Please send me one million rials," then throws them out the window. The Imam finds one of the papers and sends him 50,000 rials. He spends it all on qat and tries again: "Please send me one million rials—but not via the Imam." Rushby: "People are never happy for long." Hassan: "They become restless ... they travel. In Islam a man must travel—he must perform the hajj pilgrimage to Mecca. That is a requirement." In the tenth century, when the Sufi mystic al-Hallaj claimed that a believer could come to God without a pilgrimage to Mecca, he was tortured and killed as a heretic. Rushby: "The authorities were quite clear: the journey had to be done and no amount of meditation, with or without chemical assistance on hand, could ever take the place of that fact." That is why Rushby begins his journey in Addis Ababa, follows the tracks of Burton and Rimbaud, and crosses the gulf of Aden to Yemen, remembering as he goes Arab tales in which "the man who can hold his nerve must cross the dreadful oceans if fabulous treasures are to be discovered." Rushby is not looking for fabulous treasures, only decent quantities of qat, but oceans have to be crossed. Getting on a plane in London and flying to San'a would not have done at all.[27]

Philip Marsden's *The Chains of Heaven* is the perfect, antiphonal counterpart to *Eating the Flowers of Paradise*. Marsden, too, revisits an earlier self. In the 1980s he went to Ethiopia, then suffering under Mengistu's Red Terror, when he was a young man of twenty-one. Now, twenty years later, he returns after years of wandering and a previous book, written under a different name, that recounted his early travels in Ethiopia.[28] For him, Ethiopia means not the Islamic south but the Christian highlands of the north; not languorous, luxuriant afternoons of qat-dreaming but walking among the mountains and visiting holy places that can only be reached with extreme difficulty: *per ardua ad astra.* To the highlanders of the north, "nothing is as intrinsically bad as the *qola,* the lowlands." They are "a place of insects and diseases, big animals, dangerous Muslims and *budas*"—human devils possessed of the evil eye. In the highlands is salvation.[29]

Like a medieval pilgrim, Marsden intends to walk, despite the incredulity of an Ethiopian friend: "You can't *walk!* Foreigners don't *walk.*" But he does, covering some two hundred miles north from Lalibela and its astonishing churches to Axum, home to the Ark of the Covenant. He travels backwards in time: from twelfth-century Lalibela to fourth-century Axum. It is a journey back to beginnings, far past the catastrophe of the Red Terror to the earliest Christian world. For Philip Marsden, Ethiopian Christianity represents everything that is "extraordinary and ageless about the country.... There is nowhere on earth quite like Ethiopia."[30]

His route takes him from church to church, monastery to monastery: Yimrehanna Krestos, a twelfth-century church built within the rock, "a cave within a a cave;" Bilbala Giorgis, also twelfth-century; Bahir Kedane Mehret, a nineteenth-century monastery; Mescal Krestos, "high, high up!"—"cut into the rock by God!;" Abba Yohannis, "five hundred feet of cliff and a few holes in the rock halfway up;" Abba Salama; Mariam Korkor; and Debra Damo, oldest of them all and farthest away—another Homeric catalogue of stirring names and holy places.[31]

Abba Salama is the nearest of them to heaven: "as we drew closer, so the land between fell away, until we were standing on the edge of a dizzying chasm. The monastery was an island of rock connected to the main plateau by a broken isthmus. Even after weeks in the highlands, the scale of those cliffs was overwhelming…. The monastery cliffs rose across the gap like the gates of another world." Reaching the monastery is a pilgrim's progress. A narrow path along a ledge, empty space to one side, leads to a ladder, made up of two iron ladders welded together, that begins "at a slight angle to the vertical" and then becomes "flush and sheer with the rock face." At the top, short of the summit, the ladder stops. A nearby chain is "three or four arms' lengths away," not in reach. "You had to traverse the cliff face and make a grab for the chain," pressing fingers into handholds in the rock. "You reached the chain and gripped it," fingers slipping with sweat. "You leaned back and pulled yourself up the last twenty feet of cliff, and this was the worst part. Because this last section was overhanging." And there at the summit, the abbot of the monastery, Abbaminata Gabre-Mariam Gabre-Mikhael, is waiting: "That chain gives me so much pleasure," he says: "Look at you—sweating so much! When I climb, I just put my faith in God."[32]

After Abba Salama, it is all downhill, a diminuendo. Debra Damo is atop another sheer cliffside but lacks the acrophobic terrors of Abba Salama. A monk on the summit lets down a rope of plaited hides: "After Abba Salama, such an ascent presented few difficulties." And, once there, the pilgrim finds little beyond the ordinary: "a small town" with refectories, churches, cattle—even though, on the periphery, "your toes push out over thousands of feet of space." As for the Ark of the Covenant, "the question of whether it is actually in Aksum can be left to the myth-seekers, grail-chasers and Indiana Joneses." When he finally arrives in Axum, Marsden checks into the Africa Hotel. He wanders through the town, barely pausing to notice, behind high railings, "a monk yawning like a caged lion" who guards the entrance to the chapel that houses the Ark. He passes quickly by, not stopping (we assume) to pay the ransom-like fee demanded by the monks of St. Mary's if one wants to view, through the railing, an array of ancient (the visitor is told) gold crowns. It is a tourist trap, Ethiopian-style, and better left to Indiana Jones. Marsden himself yearns to be back on the road. His travelling companion Hiluf has rejoined his wife and daughter, and Marsden asks him, "How is it being back?" "It's fine," he says. "He was smiling his all-solving smile, but I sensed that he too already missed the open road." The open road is the pilgrim's natural home.[33]

❖   I M GOING TO ETHIOPIA : DERVLA MURPHY

The indomitable Dervla Murphy concedes the romantic origins of her journey as she heads for Ethiopia: "From earliest childhood the romantic names of Prester John, Rasselas, the Queen of Sheba and the Lion of Judah are linked with Abyssinia and, in one's reading, occasional references to the country build up a picture of some improbable land of violence and piety, courtesy and treachery, barrenness and fertility.... Often the lure of such places operates subconsciously. Then one fine morning the traveller wakes and surprises himself by saying—'I'm going to Ethiopia.'" But this story of origins is a confession of sterotypes to be overcome. What Murphy finds in the event includes no little violence, piety, courtesy, treachery, barrenness and fertility. What she leaves at home is the romance. With its plain bread-and-butter title, *In Ethiopia with a Mule* is an anti-romance, a day-by-day journal of wandering in the mountains that aims to tell it as it is. At the same time, the narrative is not lacking for a hero, Murphy's faithful Achates, the endearing mule Jock. Nor, in the long run, can she quite overlook the claims of romance.[34]

Day by day, Murphy's Ethiopia is not a land of golden legend and spiritual heights but of bugs and bandits, of squalor that is more common than splendor, the occasional hyena, and mountains as ruthless as they are exhilarating. At the end, after three months on the go, she tallies up how far she has walked; a total of 1,024 miles (perhaps 600, as the crow flies), in two separate legs: the first from Makalle in the north to Gondar and Bahir Dar; the second, after a brief interval, from Bahir Dar to Addis Ababa by way of Lalibela. Jock, exhausted, is left to recover at a village north of Addis Ababa. For the final hundred miles, Murphy takes the bus.

The journal form, with its attention to the moment, underlines the ephemeral complications and discomforts of travel: the fleas, bugs, and body-lice that infest the local huts; and "the loo-problem" that is "acute in every settlement—to my mystification, discomfort and embarrassment." Though "crude and stinking," the loo is "a worthwhile amenity," and Murphy's embarrassment lies mostly in finding it, sometimes with a "certain loss of dignity" when she has to use "sign-language" to explain her needs. In Ethiopia, unlike Nepal, "squatting just anywhere is not customary." These are complications that any traveller will recognize but not the sort that usually find their way into realms of quest and pilgrimage. Except for occasional evocations of a grand sunrise or sunset, Murphy avoids the lavish style and embraces, instead, the down-to-earth and matter-of-fact. Having struggled up the last fifty feet of Ras Dashan, at 15,158 feet the highest mountain in Ethiopia, she feels like "a fly that has just been sprayed with D.D.T."[35]

The desire to tell it the way it is sometimes inflects Murphy's account with surprising harshness: "Words fail me when it comes to describing the dreariness of Bahar Dar—so I quote from my guide-book." The prose and the picture of Bahir Dar that follow from the guide-book are certainly dispiriting, but the "hundreds of tin-roofed hovels" and the textile factory that Murphy herself adds to the picture would not distinguish Bahir Dar, in dreariness or anything else, from other African cities. Myself, I remember sitting on a hotel balcony overlooking the lake in Bahir Dar, watching bicyclists racing on a tree-lined boulevard below and thinking it was all extremely pleasant. But perhaps things have changed in the decades between Murphy's visit and my own. In any case, her dislike of Bahir Dar is more than matched by her dislike of Dessie and Addis Ababa. Dessie means "My Joy," but "never have I seen such a depressingly ugly collection of human habitations," while "Addis Ababa means 'New Flower', a misnomer that many *faranjs*"—foreigners—"find wonderfully funny. However, this malformed infant capital so atrophied my sense of humour that I never saw the joke." Her first impression of Addis Ababa is of "more tin roofs than usual"; her "permanent" impression, that of "a calamitously *unreal* city," a "faked jewel that has been hastily stuck on to the fabric of Empire." No doubt Addis Ababa is not "the real Ethiopia" any more than New York City, compared with Tennessee or Wyoming, is the real United States. Arriving in Dessie or Addis Ababa after months in the mountains, Murphy is suffering a sense of dislocation like that of Rasselas arriving in Cairo or Samuel Johnson arriving in London.[36]

For anyone inclined to Philip Marsden's view, that Ethiopian Christianity represents what is "extraordinary and ageless about the country," Murphy's account will come as a surprise: perhaps (on the one hand) as a fair corrective to the pieties of Marsden and others; perhaps (on the other) as a distorted view; but however much or little to the general point, it takes its rise in particular experience. As Murphy makes her way around the north shore of Lake Tana through inhospitable and swampy ground, four men approach her. In the lead is a priest, "nonchalantly twirling his white horse-hair fly-whisk and reverently carrying his Coptic cross." After some polite conversation, the priest tells her she must spend the night in their compound, she declines, and then the men take all her money, her camera, and most of her supplies, including "a packet of Tampax," from Jock's pack-saddle, leaving her to spend a cold, desolate night in a landscape of marsh grass, high reeds, and thorns. The priest, she learns eventually, is Kas Makonnen, a notorious *shifta*—a bandit—"wanted for countless robberies and two murders." He is also, Murphy decides when she is present at his arrest, a real priest. His partners in skullduggery are "handled brutally," but he is "allowed to sit in the shade." Small wonder that Murphy is on guard against the church and its representatives.[37]

Whether it is her encounter with Kas Makonnen or an ingrained aversion to most things religious, Murphy simply does not like much of what she sees of Ethiopian Christianity. Early on, she has breakfast with "an endearing old priest" at a "famous local church" in a village south of Axum. But she soon tires of "famous churches," their inaccessibility and, if they are accessible, their locked doors. A few days after her breakfast with the endearing priest, she finds herself on an amba where, "near the southern edge," is yet "another 'famous church'—how inaccessible can you make your famous churches! –which, as usual, was locked." Later still, in Debre Tabor, near Bahir Dar, "I did a test walk to the local 'famous church'…. The church was locked and in the nearby settlement no one would volunteer to open it. Situations like this repeatedly reveal an ingrained unhelpfulness in the highland character," an observation so much at odds with Murphy's more considered reactions to the highlanders that her crankiness seems more to do with the locked church than the unhelpfulness of the villagers.[38]

When Murphy visits Yimrehanna Krestos near Lalibela, the church within a cave that is also on Philip Marsden's pilgrimage, matters grow even worse. The priests, sounding "more like *shifta* than clergy," demand a large entrance fee, Murphy resists, they all get into a snarling match before agreeing on a lesser fee, and she is admitted to the cave, though not to the church itself. Come back tomorrow morning, she is told, and the church will be opened. In the meanwhile she explores the cave, finds a heap of "disintegrating mummies," so poorly embalmed that there are "many more skeletons than mummies." As she walks, she breaks a rib on a child's skeleton. It is a far cry from the epiphany of the Cambridge undergraduates coming into the presence of three ancient kings. In a spasm of mixed anger and sadness, Murphy sets the benevolence of the church's twelfth-century founder up against the money-grubbing of the present: "suddenly, in this remote shrine of fossilized sanctity, the moribund religion of modern Ethiopia seemed intensely tragic." The next day, when she returns, she is denied entrance to the church, perhaps because the priests fear she is on the lookout for priestly thieving of artifacts. The priests are her particular aversion: "the highland priesthood seems to attract the worst type of highlander—or rather to breed him, since the priesthood is mainly hereditary."[39]

Of Ethiopian religious festivals, "Timkat," the festival of the Epiphany in January, is most important. The tabot, a replica of the Ark of the Covenant, is carried through the streets by priests in gala dress. There is revelry, chanting, music, and dance, and Murphy can't stand any of it: "Sitting on a boulder—watching the dancing priests and the leaping laymen, and the galloping spear-throwers, and listening to drums, bells, sistra, chantings, ululations and pounding hoofs—I felt, not for the first time, an uncomfortable reaction to Ethiopian Christianity. To me there is something false about it." She concedes feeling guilty since, after all, she knows little about the Ethiopian Church. But, feeling guilty or not, she can't escape the sense, in the celebrations, of "something dead, or atrophied, or unborn." It is all a jolly holiday without "spiritual vitality," an occasion for "lots of extra food, alcohol and love-making"—but none of it related "to true worship." One may think this borderline puritanical, speculate about the love-making—seen or imagined?—and wonder whether true worship need be mystical, unworldly, but Dervla Murphy is nothing if not outspoken. That, among other things, is what journals are for.[40]

For this deracinated daughter of the Irish church, the holy city of Lalibela inspires still more mixed feelings. The churches themselves live up to their reputation: "they are among the few renowned 'wonders of the world' which, when seen at last, gave me a shock of joy." Even here one feels a lurking sense of discomfort with famous churches and wonders of the world, but Murphy capitulates to their wondrousness, quoting an early Ethiopian scribe: "He who beholds them will never be able to gaze his fill; his marvelling is so great that his heart is never tried of admiring them." Murphy: "I quite agree." Notwithstanding the wonder of the churches, however, the town of Lalibela suffers from the same infection as the priests: "the atmosphere of the town depresses me." It is no longer the remote village it once was. Tourists come and go. There is a passable hotel, for better or worse, offering "a reasonable imitation of Home Comforts." The children of the town are "a corps of professional beggars," and "the taint of greed lies heavy on the air." But where in Africa do children not beg enthusiastically?[41]

Recording her feelings as she goes, Murphy displays the usual fluctuation of human moods. Not every entry, perhaps, was penned on the spot and at the time: when, for example, did she write up the account of the robbery? It was dark, and the robbers took her ballpoint pen. But narrative immediacy is her gift, whether the subject is a moment, in the presence of a radiant moon, of "curiously disembodied … enchantment," or the "loo-problem," or the thuggery of Kas Makonnen. And in the end, she renounces her testy feelings in a retrospective view that bathes everything in romantic light. In the countryside—the real Ethiopia—outside Addis Ababa, she sees a wedding procession, "among the most charming sights I have ever seen." A little further on she comes across the wedding tent and is suddenly "seized by a pair of laughing girls and a small grinning boy." They take her into the celebration on the "most endearing assumption that naturally the passing stranger would like to join the party." Inside are dancing and singing and ululating and, when the bridegroom arrives, "all the women united to produce a beautiful trembling wave of sound that seemed to come from some invisible, far-away choir." What was missing in Timkat is notably present here in the music of an imagined, far-away choir. The least star-struck of travellers, Murphy ends her story with a traditional, pastoral wedding that heals all wounds and misapprehensions—even though, in this ceremony, the fourteen-year old bride bursts into tears when presented to her future husband; and even though the marriage-night may, according to highland custom, turn into "a semi-public test of the will-power and physical strength of both partners." Realism demands truth-telling, but the trembling wave of ethereal sound hangs in the air.[42]

Finally, as she departs, Murphy gathers the highlanders she has met along her way in a final embrace. Unhelpful villagers who won't unlock the doors of their famous local church are a remote memory, surly and dangerous priests forgotten, because the traveller has learned how to be in touch with an alien world. Though she speaks none of the local languages, "genuine communication" can be achieved, "mysteriously but unmistakably, on that basic level where ideas are excluded but sincerity of feeling has full scope," but it can be achieved, in Ethiopia "more than in any other country I know," only "unconsciously." At the wedding party, she feels herself a different person from the one who arrived in Amhara three months before, and "if these strange, aloof Tigreans and Amharas had not revealed a fundamental responsiveness, through countless tiny details, I could never have built my side of the bridge." Imbedded in the countless tiny details on which she builds her narrative, as now we realize, are marks of an unacknowledged, almost subterranean quest, sought unconsciously and unconsciously achieved, for communication, or communion, with others and with herself: "A traveller who does not speak their language cannot presume to claim any deep understanding of the Ethiopian highlanders. But it is the gradual growth of affection for another race, rather than the walking of a thousand miles or the climbing of a hundred mountains, that is the real achievement and the richest reward of such a journey." What Dervla Murphy has been looking for all along is what she found missing in the Timkat celebrations, a spiritual vitality beyond conviviality, even beyond words.[43]

CHAPTER FIVE

Remembering Zion

IN 1914, THE JAMAICAN-BORN MARCUS GARVEY, having just returned to Jamaica from London, founded the Universal Negro Improvement Association, or UNIA. Garvey was a charismatic figure, and UNIA quickly gathered membership and strength. Over 1,000 branches were established by 1920, the year when the Association held its first convention in New York. In that same year, Garvey's music director Arnold Ford—Jewish, black, born in Barbados—published his *Universal Ethiopian Hymnal,* and a resolution was offered at the convention that "the anthem 'Ethiopia, Thou Land of Our Fathers' etc. shall be the anthem of the Negro Race":

> Ethiopia, thou land of our fathers,
> Thou land where the Gods loved to be,
> As the storm cloud at night suddenly gathers
> Our armies come rushing to thee.
> We must in the fight be victorious
> When swords are thrust outward to gleam;
> For us will the victory be glorious
> When led by the red, black and green.

Red, black, and green were the colors of UNIA, recalling the green, yellow, and red of the Ethiopian flag.[1]

For centuries "Ethiopia" had meant roughly the same thing as "Africa;" and "Ethiopian," in effect, anyone of dark skin. A seventeenth-century map divided all of Africa into "higher" and "lower" Aethiopia and labeled "higher" Aethiopia—the northern half of sub-Saharan Africa—as "the empire of the Abissines." One of the swains in Shakespeare's *Love's Labours Lost* addresses his beloved: "Do not call it sin in me,/ That I am forsworn for thee;/ Thou for whom Jove would swear/ Juno but an Ethiop were." "Ethiopians" were barred at first from serving in the forces of the American Revolution. One of Arnold Ford's "Ethiopian" hymns was "O Africa awaken." And Ethiopia, "land of our fathers" in Garvey's UNIA anthem, is synonymous with the African continent. Only when Ras Tafari was crowned as Haile Selassie was the identity of Ethiopia as a nation-state fully confirmed, with the result, over time, that the larger, historic idea of "Ethiopia" gave ground to that of a particular place in a particular corner of the continent. The coronation also had a consequence that neither Evelyn Waugh nor Marcus Garvey nor Haile Selassie could possibly have foreseen: Ethiopia became the inspiration for a new religion that rooted and flowered in the tropical soil of Jamaica. Its prophet was Leonard Howell and its messiah, Haile Selassie, though it was not a role that the emperor, a serious Christian, ever embraced. Rastafarianism owed its being to Ras Tafari.[2]

Leonard Percival Howell was long a little-known and shadowy figure in Jamaican history, but that has changed with the publication in 1999 of Hélène Lee's biography, *Le Premier Rasta;* its English translation in 2003; and the publication, with commentary, of Howell's *The Promised Key* in a collection of scholarly essays, *Chanting Down Babylon: The Rastafari Reader,* in 1998. *The Promised Key,* the rarest of volumes until its printing in *Chanting Down Babylon,* is the founding text of Rastafarianism and its devotion to Haile

Selassie, called King Alpha, and his empress, Queen Omega.

The Promised Key opens with an homage to the "mystery country" of Ethiopia and a highly colored (but in some degree factual) description of preparations for the coronation—new roads, new lawns, new electric lights—and events at the ceremony itself: "Dignitaries of the world power presented King Alpha with the wealth of oceans." Then Howell presents his messianic message, echoing Solomonic and Christian traditions: "The glory that was Solomon still reigns in Ethiopia…. [O]h come let us adore him…. His Majesty Ras Tafari is the head over all man for he is the Supreme God." This Supreme God is also the adversary of the Pope of Rome, whose "agents shall not prevail against the King of Kings…. All ye warriors of the King of Kings lift high King Alpha's Royal Banner, from victory to victory King Alpha shall lead his army till every enemy is vanquished." Where did Howell come upon this visionary scene?[3]

Born in 1898, he claimed to have travelled "over a large section of the inhabited world" before returning to Jamaica in the 1930s, and it was rumored that he had attended the coronation. That is improbable. More likely, his description of the coronation gave rise to the rumor. Certainly Howell did not need first-hand knowledge, given the extent of international coverage. Whether or not he had travelled the inhabited world, he had been to Manhattan and lived in Harlem, where he clashed with the Garveyites, in the years just before and after 1930. In Harlem, he could have seen, amongst all the coronation hoopla, *Time* magazine's coverage on 3 November 1930, the day after the coronation. A head-on portrait of Haile Selassie appeared on the cover and, inside, a lengthy story. Some of it is more than a little florid: Addis Ababa is a "barbaric stronghold," evidently because it lies in "mighty mountains" at 6,000 feet. But despite the journalistic infatuation with barbaric strongholds, the story concludes reasonably enough: "Certainly the new Emperor is the greatest Abyssinian ruler of modern times. Grandeur and a fine sensitiveness are blended in his person." And: he is "waking up a land which has slept for 5,000 years." The writer seems to have remembered Edward Gibbon but not wanted to be outdone; Gibbon said the Abyssinians had slept for a thousand years.[4]

Howell might also have seen the *National Geographic* issue of June 1931, an extravaganza of reporting on things Ethiopian, especially the coronation. One article is by Addison E. Southard, the United States Minister to Ethiopia: "Modern Ethiopia: Haile Selassie the First, Formerly Ras Tafari, Succeeds to the World's Oldest Continuously Sovereign Throne." The article runs to almost sixty pages of text and photographs, not counting the sixteen pages of "natural color photographs" by staff photographer W. Robert Moore, who contributed a second article: "Coronation Days in Addis Ababa." After an account of the coronation, Southard turns to the history and customs of the country, "fascinating Ethiopia," pausing even to ponder and then downgrade the old story of Ethiopian fondness for raw meat: "raw-meat eating is largely ceremonial." At the center of everything, however, are the color photographs: of the abuna who crowned the emperor; of the Minister of War in full regalia riding "a gaily-caparisoned mule"; of two "Amharic belles"; of local street scenes and landscapes; of the American delegation to the coronation; of "the lion of the tribe of Judah in coronation raiment"; and, first of the color plates, "the newly-crowned monarchs of historic Ethiopia"—the emperor and empress in red and gold coronation robes and sumptuous crowns, the emperor bearing orb and scepter, their two sons on either side. The portrait is "posed especially," we are told, "for the National Geographic Society's representative." The image is blurred. The light at the coronation had been insufficient for color photography, and the emperor "kindly consented" to a posed version; but, Moore explains, "many delays" intervened and he finally took the photograph just before leaving Addis Ababa, late one afternoon as light was "rapidly failing." The result is a gaudy, atmospheric blur of red and gold.[5]

Haile Selassie was the right emperor, in the right place, at the right time. The Psalmist (68: 31) had prophesied, "Princes shall come out of Egypt; Ethiopia shall soon stretch out her hands to God," and "Ethiopianism" had grown and flowered in the decade after Garvey founded UNIA. Proclaiming that Ras Tafari was the Supreme God, Leonard Howell had grasped the main chance. He and his followers created a commune called "Pinnacle," high in the hills above the old capital of Spanish Town. It was burned by local authorities in 1958, and its members dispersed to the shacks and shanties of Kingston. The religion of Ras Tafari now had what new religions need: direct experience of oppression, in this case merging with the historic oppression of blacks by whites. "Ironically," as Hélène Lee says, but not surprisingly, "the Jamaican police had succeeded only in spreading the 'Rasta Menace' they were trying to suppress," the same irony that marked early Christianity or the death of the Mormon martyr Joseph Smith.[6]

New religions also need a sacred text if they are to flourish, and *The Promised Key,* if only on account of its scarcity, might not have fulfilled that need. The true sacred text of Rastafarianism became that of reggae music, especially but not only that of Bob Marley. "By the Rivers of Babylon," originally by the Melodians, sets the language of Psalm 137 to music to express the feelings of the Jamaican diaspora: "By the rivers of Babylon,/ Where he sat down,/ And there he wept/ When he remembered Zion./ Oh, the wicked carried us away captivity,/ Required from us a song,/ How can we sing King Alpha's song/ In a strange land?" The Psalmist's "songs of Zion" become those of "King Alpha," the dispossessed are far from his kingdom, and so—in the words of Psalm 19:14—"let the words of our mouth/ And the meditations of our heart/ Be acceptable in thy sight./ Oh, verai." If the songs of Zion are recast as King Alpha's, the Lord of the Israelites, "my strength and my redeemer," is made mysterious: in other transcriptions the last words are not "Oh, verai" but "Over I" and "Here tonight." Given the secret language common in Rastafarian speech, especially the quirky use of the first person, the best guess may be "Over I."[7]

But it was the inexhaustible Marley, in song after song and album after album, who broadcast the gospel of Ras Tafari and Ethiopia around the world, intertwining the gospel and the secular, love songs and Rasta chants, all proclaiming the music's redemptive power. "Is This Love" celebrates the love of Jah, God of the Rastafarians, for his chosen people: "I wanna love you, and treat you right/ I wanna love you, every day and every night / We'll be together, with a roof right over our heads/ We'll share the shelter, of my single bed/ We'll share the same room, JAH provide the bread." "Chanting Down Babylon" is a ritual incantation: "And how I know, and that's how I know/ A Reggae Music, mek we chant down Babylon/ With music, mek we chant down Babylon/ This music, mek we chant down Babylon/ This music, come we chant down Babylon." And again: "Come we go chant down Babylon one more time/ Come we go chant down Babylon one more time/ For them soft, yes them soft/ Them soft, mi say them soft/ So come we go chant down Babylon one more time." Liturgical repetition commingles with secular refrain. The words and music of Marley's songs constitute one answer to Dervla's Murphy's complaint that alcohol—or, in Marley's case, ganja—and love-making have nothing to do with spirituality and true worship.

If not for Marley and the music of reggae, Rastafarianism would not have travelled the world as it has. It has migrated to other islands of the Caribbean, to the United States, Canada, Britain, Europe, Australia, New Zealand, and several Pacific islands. Marley T-Shirts turn up everywhere, in Shanghai and Calcutta, Marrakech and Brazzaville, Jakarta and Recife; and Marley has become a presence in the world pantheon of spiritual heroes: in the American southwest, he is venerated by the Havasupai Indians; in Nepal, some believe he is an incarnation of Vishnu, the god of a thousand names; on a mountainside in Peru, a legend is carved: "Bob Marley"—not Elvis, another musical incarnation of the godhead—"is King." How many of these worshippers, like punters at the Happy Valley Racecourse in Hong Kong, are aware of their starting point, and Bob Marley's, in ancient Abyssinia?[8]

If the believers' gene is missing in one's own make-up, it will be hard to believe in some beliefs, for example that anyone could actually think that Haile Selassie or Jesus or Bob Marley—or a certain John Frum, the mythical American soldier whose messianic return is expected in Vanuatu—is God's avatar. But there is no doubting Marley's faith. In April 1966, the emperor and a large official party visited Jamaica. So tumultuous was the scene at the airport that the emperor refused to leave the plane until he received assurances from a Rastafarian leader that he could do so safely. Bob Marley was out of the country at the time, but his wife Rita was among the many thousands looking on. Though it was Leonard Howell who began it all, it was Rita Marley's visionary imagination, as the emperor drove through the streets of Kingston, that sealed the future. As she would tell the story, he turned, waved, looked directly at her, and on his hands she saw stigmata, the evidence of divinity. She wrote Bob, telling him what she had seen. When he returned to Jamaica, the great musical days of the new religion lay just ahead.[9]

In an introduction to Hélène Lee's biography of Howell, Stephen Davis remembers interviewing Marley in 1973 while he was on tour in Boston: "he was much more interested in talking about being a Rastafarian than he was about selling reggae music." As to the main article of his faith, Marley is memorably matter-of-fact: he "quietly said that he and the band thought that the Ethiopian emperor, Haile Selassie I, was a living god." Then he "looked me in the eye and quoted the lyric he and Peter Tosh were singing every night to ecstatic audiences...: 'We know and we over-stand, Almighty God is a living man.'" Davis, a prolific journalist of the musical scene in the 1960s and 1970s, does not hide his skepticism yet seems to admit some willing suspension of disbelief in the presence of Marley's solid assurance: "For the next three years, Bob Marley fenced with his many interviewers about his deeply held faith. Yes, he told them, Haile Selassie was 'Jah, Rastafari, who liveth and reigneth I-tinually.'" In one of his songs, the lyrics come verbatim from an anti-imperialist speech by the emperor. In the long run, however, the Rasta faith holds above all that salvation lies in going home. Davis describes another conversation with Marley: "'Yeah, mon,' he told me one night, bored with my skepticism, 'Rasta must go home to Africa,'" as Marcus Garvey had preached and, for that matter, as Rasselas and the others had done, after their time of exile, in Johnson's fiction. The emperor and Ethiopia are an embodiment of home, as Abyssinia was for Samuel Johnson's prince and princess two centuries before.[10]

The politics of Rasta, the divisions and contests that marked the 1970s, especially after the death of the emperor, do not matter here, but Marley's 1980 baptism in the Ethiopian Orthodox church implies the question, how to reconcile the divinity of the emperor and the divinity of Jesus? When Marley joined the church, was he surrendering one faith for another? Hélène Lee thinks that he was: "Why did Bob Marley turn his back on the Rastas?" And: "Perhaps he wanted to please his mother, who had been trying for years to bring him back to Christianity. For the Rastas, however, it was a blow. Their ambassador, their prince, had gone to die in the arms of Jesus." Though Hélène Lee is better able than I to assess the effects of Marley's decision, the issue, on her own evidence, was more secular and political than spiritual: "In front of whom could he have bent his head, when each and every Rasta leader sought nothing but favors?" And, on the spiritual side of things—in lay terms, the psychological side—Marley's near-death baptism seems an extension, not a repudiation, of a belief system in which the stigmata that Rita Marley saw on the emperor's hands mingled with dreams of an African Zion. In 1961, a Jamaican "back-to-Africa mission," the brain-child of Prime Minister Norman Manley, had travelled to several African nations and found, in Ethiopia, yet another happy valley, the stretch of land 125 miles south of Addis Ababa that Haile Selassie had offered Western blacks who wished to settle there. The delegation, entranced, reported that the land was "beautiful rolling country that lies between the Malkoda and Shashamani rivers on the lower slopes of the Addis plateau." "Word of Shashamani," Lee reports, "hit Jamaica like Paradise Found," and a few Rastas actually managed to make their way there. A modern guide book, which calls Shashamani "a mushrooming amorphous clutter of ugly buildings and leering, loutish youths," also notes the remnants of a reclusive Rastafarian community nearby. Dreams of Zion die hard. Bob Marley's baptism had less to do with dying in the arms of Jesus than in the arms of the motherland.[11]

Many thousands of Jamaicans, including the Prime Minister and the opposition leader, took part in Marley's funeral and followed a motorcade to Nine Mile, the small, rural hamlet in the mountains where he was born. His remains lie in an elegant, simple mausoleum perched on flattened land atop a small hill, as if in imitation of an Ethiopian amba. But that is not the very end of the story. In February 2005, the sixtieth anniversary of Marley's birth, a full month of celebrations took place in Ethiopia. The main event was a concert, eagerly anticipated, in Meskel Square in the heart of Addis Ababa. Ethiopia's minister of state for information issued an official welcome: "Bob Marley put Ethiopia on a pedestal and it is in his honour that this festival is going to take place here." Notices were posted on the Web, including one by "an Abyssinian Boy": "I'm an Abyssinian Boy, True Jahnoy Lijj. mi live inna Ethiopia. and I really waiting for that day. FEBRUARY 6, we gonna blaze da fire in Meskel Square. Addis Ababa is look like a beautiful girl now. Everyone is waiting for dat day." After the concert, the celebration moved on to the Ethiopian home of the Rastas, Shashamani.[12]

But there was controversy, too. Locally, the Rastas in Shashamani used the moment to protest the seizure of their land by Mengistu's regime and their lack of full citizenship. In Jamaica, there was dismay over Rita Marley's intention—in accord, she said, with her husband's wishes—to take his body from Nine Mile for re-burial in Ethiopia. Whether Rastas had been troubled or, as I suppose, mostly not, by Bob Marley's conversion to Ethiopian Christianity, and even though "back-to-Africa" had been a rallying call, the thought of his leaving Jamaica provoked a storm, and Rita stepped back: "It was a dream of Bob Marley and it is a dream of the family to bury him in Ethiopia. As we believe in what is to be, must be, it will happen in due course." But only in due course, whenever that might turn out to be.[13]

On 1 February 2005, the British Broadcasting Company posted some questions on the Web: "Should Bob Marley be reburied in Ethiopia? How would you feel if you were Jamaican? Do you think Ethiopians and other Africans should support the Marley family's wish to rebury him in Ethiopia?" Responses came from around the globe. All three postings from Jamaica were firmly against: "If it was really Bob's wish to be buried in Ethiopia why didn't they bury him there in the first instance"; and, "I think it would be devastating and disappointing if one of our most beloved sons were to be taken away from us"; and, "Bob's remains must remain in Jamaica." A single posting came from Addis Ababa—"No problem we will welcome"— and another from an Ethiopian living in Michigan: "It is an honour for the people of Ethiopia to rebury Bob in Ethiopia, if it is possible next to nation's Father Emperor Haile Selassie's grave." Opinions from the African continent—Kenya, Uganda, Zimbabwe, Nigeria, Zambia, Cameroon, Malawi, South Africa—were mixed. One posting, from Kenya, said that "his remains should be left in peace;" another, from South Africa, that "in this age of African unity, why shouldn't Bob Marley be buried in the land of his fathers?" Another, from Zambia, said that "his reburial in Ethiopia is besides the point;" and still another, with a political edge, from Zimbabwe: "Ethiopia has been about oppression for as long as anyone can remember. Wars, famines, disease, political unrest, uncaring government…, the most uncouth rulers. How then can anyone want to associate that with Bob Marley?" Other returns, equally mixed in their views, came from Croatia, Estonia, South America, New York City, Britain. "Mike," giving his address only as "England," wrote: "It's a dead body, who really cares?"[14]

Of course it was Jamaica that really cared. Roger Steffens, not Jamaican but a friend of Marley's and a historian of his music, called the plan "an appalling development for Jamaica" and denied that Bob ever wanted to be buried in Ethiopia: "The country that created the faith of Rastafari is Jamaica, not Ethiopia." In this unedifying squabble, the village of Nine Mile stood to lose the most, for Marley's grave, like that of Jim Morrison at Père Lachaise in Paris, has become a tourist destination and is a source of revenue for an otherwise impoverished outpost. A Web site calling itself "Reggae.com" announced that "this would be a sad betrayal of Bob, Jamaica and fans of his music and message whose seed grew out of fertile soil in Jamaica." It also offered a link to a Nine Mile site with a commercial pitch: "As many have found, a trip to Nine Mile renews faith in some of the important elements of life…. On your journey to Nine Mile you will enjoy breathtaking views while absorbing the natural beauty of the tranquil Jamaican countryside…. Nine Mile is owned and operated by Bob's family. It is not unusual to find his mother, affectionately called Mother B, personally greeting visitors, sometimes even being persuaded to relate stories of her son's childhood." Commerce is the way of the world, and the declension of belief into commerce is no new story. Johnson's happy Abyssinian valley turns into a landscape of laundromats and racecourses; Bob Marley's dream of Zion, into a theme park. "Regular tours are available," says the Nine Mile site, "from Montego Bay, Ocho Rios, Negril, and Kingston. Hotel pick-up is available."[15]

We need not begrudge the residents of Nine Mile their good fortune. As for Ethiopia and Jamaica, perhaps the claims of each can be accommodated. In 1997, St. Martin's Press published *The Kebra Nagast; The Lost Bible of Rastafarian Wisdom and Faith from Ethiopia and Jamaica*. Accommodation is the goal: "from Ethiopia and

Jamaica." Bound in faux morocco and lettered in gold, the jacket looks biblical, as if designed for a motel room. Inside, the text is red-letter, the headings in black—a bible for an alternative religion. The editor was Gerald Hausman, author of books for young adults, including collaborations with Cedella Marley, Bob's oldest daughter. Bob's son Ziggy provides an introduction. And the hybrid text, as promised, marries the ancient wisdom of the Kebra Nagast to the faith of Rastafarian Jamaica, on the one hand borrowing from Budge's translation, on the other telling Rasta stories and pronouncing the gospel according to Bob Marley: "Of the many prophets of Rasta, there is only one who stands out as the cornerstone of today's faith. He is a man like Solomon, a man so gifted, so wise. He is compared with Joseph of Egypt. He is called the one who sits at the right hand of Selassie I. Bob Marley is named a prophet." He has quarried the Bible and "the oral teachings of the Ethiopian elders, which come from the Kebra Nagast," and made them all his own. The two Zions come together in him.[16]

POSTLUDE: *Very Fast Running*

ABEBE BIKILA, THEN AN UNKNOWN RUNNER, startled the world in the summer of 1960 by winning the Olympic marathon in Rome. I had just made a long trip myself, a cross-county drive, New Jersey to California. A new life was waiting, which is probably what sharpens my memories of Bikila's victory. Even more startling than his win, he did it running barefoot. The commentator for the BBC was amazed: "It's an astonishing sight, I must say: the Ethiopian, Bikila Abebe, is racing barefoot!" Afterwards, Bikila made the most of it. "I wanted the world to know," he said, "that my country, Ethiopia, has always won with determination and heroism." Meanwhile, in Addis Ababa, Sylvia Pankhurst was weeks from death, but if she knew of Bikila's victory, she was surely delighted. She would not, however, have been surprised, having reminded readers of the *New Times* in 1941 that knitting socks for the soldiers was unnecessary because "Ethiopian warriors march bare-foot" and "sure-footed as the chamois they have defended their ancient heights these five years."[1]

Bikila repeated his victory in Tokyo in 1964, becoming the only runner ever to win two Olympic marathons and once again setting a world record. In 1968, a car crash ended his running career, and he spent the rest of his life in a wheelchair. But he had opened the gates. In the years since, Ethiopian runners, both men and women, have often been the best in the world: Mamo Wolde, Miruts Yifter, Derartu Tulu, Fatuma Roba, Tirunesh Dibaba, Haile Gebrselassie—called the greatest distance runner ever, and Gebrselassie's protégé, Kenenisa Bekele: a final Homeric roll call. The real history of Ethiopia over the last decades has been one of extreme hardship: fierce political oppression, wars, drought, famine. But the great runners help keep old legends alive.

Notes

Prelude: Jamaica, 1981

1. Boot and Salewicz 12, 17.

Chapter One: The Call of Abyssinia: Father Lobo, Samuel Johnson and *Rasselas*

1. Ludolf's volume was not the first to introduce Ethiopia to English-speaking readers. Narratives by Portuguese and French travellers had been translated in 1625 and 1709, and a volume by the Portuguese Balthasar Telles had been translated as *The Travels of the Jesuits in Ethiopia in 1710*. (Kolb, "Introduction" xxix; Gold xxxv). But Ludolf's history was a milestone. For the legend of Prester John, see Silverberg.

2. The table of contents of that first edition gave the title as "The History of Rasselas, Prince of Abissinia." In 1768, the first American edition, published in Philadelphia by the radical Irish bookseller and printer Robert Bell, appeared as *The History of Rasselas, Prince of Abissinia. An Asiatic Tale.* It was not until Joseph Wenman's edition of 1787 that the text appeared in London under what is now its standard title. "Abissinia" became "Abyssinia" in an 1801 London edition, though the new spelling was not stabilized until later in the nineteenth century. For the complete bibliographical history through 1984, see Fleeman 785–989.

3. Boswell 595; Gold xxiv

4. Johnson, *A Voyage* 3

5. An inference—but I think inescapable, even though *Rasselas* and Abyssinia never come directly into view in *A Journey to the Western Islands*. E.g., at the waterfall of Fiers: "The country at the bridge strikes the imagination with all the gloom and grandeur of Siberian solitude. The way makes a flexure, and the mountains, covered with trees, rise at once on the left hand and in the front" (33). Or: "Mountainous countries commonly contain the original, at least the oldest race of inhabitants, for they are not easily conquered" (43). Or: "Regions mountainous and wild, thinly inhabited, and little cultivated, make a great part of the earth, and he that has never seen them, must live unacquainted with much of the face of nature, and with one of the great scenes of human existence" (40). It is as though Johnson is (at last) living through an experience and observing a landscape that he had prefigured years earlier in his imagination.

6. Johnson mistranslates his original at this point, twice substituting the first person for LeGrand's impersonal "on." As Gold says, the "first-person account produces an effect very different from that of the French" (Johnson, *A Voyage* 46n2). Perhaps Johnson was happy to have sighted, vicariously, a unicorn.

7. Johnson, *A Voyage* 93, 33, 46, 48, 35

8. Johnson, *A Voyage* 82, 84, 83, 84–85

9. Johnson, *The Rambler* 3: 297, 3: 304

10. Boswell 240; Ludolf 28, 29; Burke 58

11. Boswell 415; Nicolson 277, 280

12. Johnson, *Rasselas* 9, 8

13. Johnson, *Rasselas* 60; Burke 72

14. Johnson, *Rasselas* 61

15. Johnson, *Rasselas* 64; Johnson, *Adventurer* 67, in *The Idler and the Adventurer* 384, 387. Gwin Kolb remarks the correspondence between the travellers' first experience of Cairo and that of Johnson's newcomer to London (Johnson, *Rasselas* 64n2).

16. Johnson, *Rasselas*, Chapter XVI header

17. Johnson, *Rasselas*, Chapter XLIX header; 175, 175–76; Boswell 240–41; *Rasselas* 176.

18. Cf. Kolb, "Textual Cruxes in *Rasselas*."

19. Johnson, *Rasselas* 10

Chapter Two: "Going Native": James Bruce, Mansfield Parkyns, Richard Burton

1. Lawrence, *Seven Pillars* 31–32

2. *Imperial Archive*

3. Halsband 326, 327

4. Grundy lists sources criticizing Montagu (139n12). Chard notices Montagu's sense that the naked women are as fascinated by her as she is by them; "the spectacle," as Chard puts it, "stares back" (156–8).

5. Grundy 139

6. Curling 38, 39, 118, 159

7. Curling 197

8. Curling 207, Bredin 262

9. Bredin 254; Bruce 3: 426, 3: 426–27

10. Bruce 3: 597, 3: 598, 3: 640, 3: 640–41

11. Pindar 2: 170

12. Geertz's method of "thick description," which teased out the logic of cultural practices and representations, is famously on display in his collection of

essays, *The Interpretation of Cultures* (1973). His analysis of the Balinese cockfight in that book's concluding piece has become a classic of anthropological writing, with notable influence over the human sciences from ethnography to literary criticism.

13. Bruce 3: 301

14. Bruce 3: 301, 3: 302, 3: 303

15. Bruce 3: 304, 3: 302, 3: 304–05. On the banquet as "a grotesque parody both of civil decorum and eucharistic ritual," cf. Leask 91ff.

16. A minor example of a recurrent orthographic problem with transliterated names, whose difficulties tripped up even the formidable Sylvia Pankhurst: "Ozero, as spelt by Bruce, is a feminine title equivalent to Lady, Miss or Mrs; it is written Waizero by most English authors" (385n). But Bruce spells the name "Ozoro." For more on transliteration, see note 34 below.

17. Bredin 125, 116

18. Bruce 3: 729

19. Bruce 3: 544, 3: 544–45, 3: 545

20. Bruce 3: 728, 3: 729, 3: 730

21. Bruce 3: 743, 3: 743–44

22. Bruce 4: 6, 4: 8; Boyle 158; Bruce 4: 9

23. Bruce 4: 369, 4: 370, 4: 405

24. Bruce's *Travels* were published in five volumes in Edinburgh and London in 1790 and in six volumes in Dublin in 1790–91. Some copies of the first volume include a portrait of Bruce and a defensive "Ode to James Bruce, Esq. By an Unknown Hand." (Might the unknown hand have beeen Bruce's own?) Abridged editions appeared in London and New York in 1790, as did a French translation in Paris (with a false "Londres" imprint on the title page). Thereafter it was frequently reprinted in English through the nineteenth century, in various redacted forms—attesting to the book's persistent appeal to readers, whatever they may have thought of its truth-value.

25. Bredin 57; Beckingham 11; Bredin 263. Henry Dufton, no lover of the Abyssinian character, wrote in the 1860s of eating flesh "warm and quivering from the ox" and of other distressing culinary habits that he had observed (206), concluding that he had no difficulty accepting Bruce's account.

26. Johnson, *The Rambler* 1: 320

27. Cumming 4, 150, 154, 163

28. Parkyns 1:13, 1:14

29. Parkyns 1:15

30. Parkyns 1:81, 1:23

31. Parkyns 1: 13, 1: 15

32. Parkyns 2: 150, 2: 151

33. Parkyns 2: 25, 2: 62, 2: 5, 2: 7. Some years ago, on the first day when mar-

riages could be performed after the Christmas season, my wife and I sat in the lobby of the Addis Ababa Hilton, surrounded by celebrating brides and bridesmaids (and probably bridegrooms as well). I would not dispute the judgment of Bruce, Parkyns, and Parkyns's expert connoisseur.

34. Here is an instance of an ongoing difficulty: the orthography of transliterated names. Should the ancient city in the north (for example) be Axum—or Aksum? Should the sacred text of Ethiopia be the *Kebra Nagast,* the *Kebra Negast,* or the *Kibre Negest?* Haile Selassie or Haile Sellassie? Mt. Wachni, Mt. Wehni, Mt. Weheni? In a learned consideration of the question, the editors of *Language in Ethiopia* remark that in such things "no one is ever fully satisfied"—and adopt their own conventions, newly formulated, "with a feeling of relief but not of enthusiasm" (Bender et al xviii). I have generally used the most familiar or common spellings, as represented (for example) in Briggs's *Guide to Ethiopia,* but in citations I have taken the orthography as it comes. This results in some disjunctions, as here. "Rohabeita" is Cumming's version; "Rohabaita," Parkyns's.

35. Cumming 69; Parkyns I: 231, I: 223, I: 232. For this information and more I am grateful to my friend Ann Schlee. She was Ann Cumming when we met first, but I did not know then of her father's diplomatic role in Eritrea and Ethiopia. Among her fictions for young adults is *The Guns of Darkness* (1974), a narrative, as told by the daughter of the Englishman John Bell and his Ethiopian wife, at the time of Tewodros. Among her later novels is *The Time in Aderra* (1996), the story of a young woman in "Aderra," a "tiny British Protectorate," at the moment when it will soon be turned over to "indigenous rule."

36. Cumming 79
37. Pratt 86, 95, 97
38. Pankhurst, "Mahbuba;" Starkie 388, 415, 395; Cumming 79; Swift 3: 103
39. Lovell discredits the story as, most of it, "demonstrably myth" (744). I think this is too decisive. However exaggerated the story may have been, we do not know exactly what, or if indeed anything, was burnt; the only evidence would have lain in ashes.
40. Starkie 13; Lovell 744ff.
41. I take the term "Greater Ethiopia" from Levine.
42. Burton I: 1–2
43. Regarding the epithet of Mohammed Gragne, the "'left-handed' Attila of Adel," Burton writes that "'Gragne,' or in the Somali dialect 'Guray,' means a left-handed man; Father Lobo errs in translating it 'the Lame'" (2: 5n). As Kolb points out, the error is in fact Johnson's mistranslation of the French *gauche* (Johnson, *A Voyage* 63n2).
44. Burton 2: 7n; Johnson, *A Voyage* 63n2
45. Burton 2: 15, I: 209, I: 206; James 4: 250

46. Burton 2: 16, 2: 17, 2: 18

47. Burton's presented his fanciful hypothesis of a geographical "sotadic zone," in which pederasty and homosexuality were especially common, in an appendix to his translation of *The Arabian Nights* (1885).

48. Brodie 205, 292; Lovell 164; Waterfield 285–86

49. On the anthropological encounter with the sexuality of others, see Lyons & Lyons. On sexuality in the field, see Ashkenazi & Markowitz.

50. Ashkenazi and Markowitz 2

51. Burton 2: 31

52. Burton 2: 34, 2: 42

Interlude: Maqdala

1. For Henty and Stanley as war correspondents, see Hoover.

2. See Acton.

3. In the Stanford University Libraries' copy, a knowledgeable reader has made some marginal corrections. "Engard," for example, is corrected to "enjara."

4. Eliot, *ODNB;* Hotten 10, 11. The British romance with Abyssinia was never so severely tested as at the time of Maqdala. Roger Acton, special correspondent for the *Illustrated London News* (though he seems never to have left his desk in London), accused the Abyssinians of all manner of laziness, vanity, and license (3). Henry Dufton, also writing at the time of the crisis, reported that "pride is not their only fault; they are deceitful, lying, insincere" (92). For a full history and bibliography of sources concerning the Maqdala episode, see Bates. The orthographical question turns up here once more: "Magdala" is the customary transliteration, as in Bates, but "Meqdala" and "Maqdala" are also found. My choice of "Maqdala" is arbitrary enough and stems from a sense that, metaphorically speaking, the exotic nature of the whole story is suggested by the aberrant "q."

5. *The Times* 11; Hotten 1–2

6. Hotten 6–7, 6

7. Zander 79

8. According to Acton, Zander was never a prisoner but, with Waldmeier and others, one of Tewodros's "hired and favoured servants" (71).

9. *Crockford's* 642

10. *Publishers' Weekly* 1 February 1890: 147; *Literary World* 21 July 1888: 234; for attributions to Veitch in *The Scottish Review*, see Houghton, 790ff. Her subjects included religious fiction, Scottish fiction, George Eliot, and—in reaction to a major craze of the time—the "fallacies of reading lists."

11. Bates 1, 218-20

Chapter Three: Barbaric Splendors and Golden Legends: Wilfred Thesiger, Evelyn Waugh, Sylvia Pankhurst

1. "Bay Area Author;" *Once upon a Romance;* Hotten 7
2. Rey 12
3. Thesiger, *The Life of My Choice* 55
4. Thesiger, *The Life of My Choice* 56
5. Thesiger, *The Life of My Choice* 64
6. Maitland 68, 75
7. Maitland 79. On the Danakil, see Nesbitt. First published in Britain as *Desert and Forest: The Exploration of the Abyssinian Danakil* (1934), Nesbitt's volume was then published in the United States (1935), by the staid firm of Alfred A. Knopf, as *Hell-Hole of Creation: The Exploration of the Abyssinian Danakil.*
8. Maitland 93–94
9. Thesiger, *The Life of My Choice* 122; Thesiger, *Danakil Diary* 67; *The Life of My Choice* 122, 123
10. I am grateful to Alexander Maitland for information, received after the first, private printing of this volume, about Thesiger's findings in the Danakil. Thesiger reported that he used a local informant, with the assistance of his Somali guide and guardian Umar, who translated for him and "joined in the discussion and asked questions."
11. Thesiger, *The Life of My Choice* 55; Maitland 57
12. Thesiger, *The Life of My Choice* 402, 440, 441
13. Kapuściński 5; Kaufman C14
14. Thesiger, *The Life of My Choice* 43
15. Maitland 435; Thesiger, *The Life of My Choice* 15
16. For the story of Clapperton, Denham and others who explored Western Africa and the Niger River region in the early 1820s, see Bovill, 71–148.
17. Thesiger, *The Life of My Choice* 92; Patey 81; Thesiger, *The Life of My Choice* 92
18. Waugh, *Essays, Articles and Reviews* 118
19. Patey 90; Waugh, *Diaries* 332; Patey, 377n17; Waugh, *Diaries* 332; Patey 90
20. Waugh, *Remote People* 20, 50, 52
21. Waugh, *Remote People* 52
22. Thesiger, *The Life of My Choice* 91; Waugh, *Remote People* 45–46, 22
23. Thesiger, *The Life of My Choice* 91
24. Waugh, *Black Mischief* 9
25. Shaw published *The Intelligent Woman's Guide to Socialism and Capitalism* in 1927. Eleanor Rathbone, a member of Parliament for the English universities, was an ardent and outspoken feminist who, like Pankhurst, took up the anti-Fascist cause in the 1930s.
26. *Waugh in Abyssinia* 8, 10

27. *Waugh in Abyssinia* 5, 6, 7, 6

28. Waugh, *Essays, Articles and Reviews* 104, 103, 104; Patey 141

29. *Waugh in Abyssinia* 33, 34, 241; Thesiger, *The Life of My Choice* 24. Addis Ababa was founded by Emperor Menelik II in 1887 and, according to tradition, named by his wife, Queen Taytu (Pankhurst, *The Ethiopians* 195).

30. *Waugh in Abyssinia* 243, 245, 253

31. Waugh, *When the Going Was Good* ix, xi, x; Patey 242

32. *Waugh in Abyssinia* 216; *New Times* 15 March 1941: 4, 12 June 1954: 4.

33. Truth in sourcing requires a confession here. I am as sure as possible that I came across this information in the *New Times and Ethiopia News*. But neither I nor my eagle-eyed helper Matthew Garrett has been able to locate the source in the process of checking references. This experience is not at all uncommon in the trade of scholarship. But it is only after decades in the business that I have an inclination to admit it.

34. *New Times* 24 August 1940: 1

35. Wrong 118; Richard Pankhurst, *Sylvia Pankhurst* 217, 236; Wrong 147

36. I rely on the bibliography assembled by her son, Richard Pankhurst, in *Sylvia Pankhurst* (260).

37. *New Times* 16 July 1955: 1

38. *New Times* 5 May 1956: 2

39. *New Times* 6 June 1936: 3

40. "Abyssinian Legends" 360

41. *New Times* 15 August 1936: 8

42. *New Times* 19 September 1936: 1

43. Wheeler 5, 25; *New Times* 19 September 1936: 1

44. Sylvia Pankhurst, *Ethiopia* 60–97, 151–152, 98, 100, 105

45. *New Times* 5 May 1956: 6, 8

46. Wrong, 118; Morris xxiii; Romero 24

Chapter Four: "I'm Going to Ethiopia": Recent Visitors

1. Wrong x

2. Frye 162, 186

3. Subject matter and emphasis in these volumes run from wildlife ecology, mountain climbing and mountain exploration, teaching in Ethiopian schools, adventuring on the Blue Nile, Jewish traditions of the Falasha, and film-making, to political history; and, in the volumes that I look at specifically, undergraduate frolics, the *Rasselas* story, the mines of Solomon, Ethiopian monasticism, the culture of qat, and wandering for the pure sake of wandering—all of these latter narratives representing not only the persistence of Ethiopian enchantment but also facets of the modern that characterize travel (and other) narratives more generally.

4. Frye 187
5. Ferguson 17, 21, 126
6. Ferguson 18, 14, 11
7. Ferguson 126
8. Ferguson 163, 165, 166, 168
9. Pakenham, *Mountains of Rasselas* 10, 13
10. Pakenham, *Mountains of Rasselas* 67
11. Pakenham, *Mountains of Rasselas* 78, 101, 102
12. Pakenham, *Mountains of Rasselas* 155, 158, 160
13. Pakenham, *Mountains of Rasselas* 187, 188
14. Pakenham, *Mountains of Rasselas* 191
15. Pakenham 192. Twelve years after Pakenham's *Mountains of Rasselas,* Barbara Toy told the story of her journey from Tunis to Ethiopia, across the Sahara, south through the Central African Republic, east through Congo, then north and finally crossing the western border of Ethiopia from Khartoum. The climax comes when, with the aid of a daring helicopter pilot, she stands on top of Mount Wehni—"I was alone on Wahni, the first European to stand on this ground, and the fact was curiously elating" (228). She spends a cold, wet night there and discovers that she is not wholly alone. She sees droppings of a carnivorous animal, probably a leopard. She thinks she hears a voice. Vultures circle expectantly. She sleeps fitfully, sensing an animal nearby. But the spectral scene gives way, at dawn, to an Elysian prospect: "as I coaxed a fire with the damp twigs, the colours heightened all around me. The valley was more beautiful than ever" (234).

In 2002, a round-the-world climbing team, sponsored by Hot Rock climbs, ascended Mount Wehni. The team claimed not only that they were first "to climb to the summit" but also, overlooking Toy's helicopter exploit, that "we are the first known people to be on the summit since it was the prison to 200 princes 300 years ago." (Climbhotrock.com)

16. Shah, *In Search* 1, 14
17. Shah, *In Search* 17
18. Shah, *In Search* ix, 44, 42
19. Shah, *In Search* 203, 214, 215, 229
20. Shah, *In Search* 232, 233
21. Bartleet, facing page 113; Shah, *In Search* 207, 208, 46, 208
22. Rushby, *Eating* 2
23. Rushby, *Eating* 16, 68
24. Rushby, *Eating* 194–95
25. Rushby, *Eating* 203
26. Rushby, *Eating* 300, 305, 309, 311, 309

27. Rushby, *Eating* 309, 310, 144
28. Marsden's *A Far Country: Travels in Ethiopia* (1990), was published under the name Philip Marsden-Smedley.
29. Marsden 42
30. Marsden 22, 23
31. Marsden 44, 135, 166
32. Marsden 189, 190, 193, 194
33. Marsden 251, 222, 296, 298
34. Murphy 1
35. Murphy 237, 56, 110
36. Murphy 170, 244, 268, 270
37. Murphy 155, 157, 172, 175
38. Murphy 66, 75, 197
39. Murphy 229, 231, 230, 231
40. Murphy 121, 122
41. Murphy 225
42. Murphy 194, 272, 275
43. Murphy 276

Chapter Five: Remembering Zion

1. Murrell et al 44; Garvey 140–41; Barrett 80
2. Shakespeare IV.3.113–16; Murrell et al 41
3. Murrell et al 365, 368, 369
4. Murrell et al 361; Lee 32–33; *Time* 23, 24
5. Southard 690, 725, 692, 697, 698, 693, 692, 691, 746
6. Murrell et al 42; Lee 4
7. Digital Tradition Mirror
8. Thirdfield.com; Murrell et al 178ff.; Davis ix; Lee ix; Murrell et al 264
9. Murrell et al 256
10. Lee vii, viii
11. Lee 288, 289, 288, 262; Briggs 217
12. BBC; Melodymakers.de
13. BBC
14. BBC
15. Mitchell, "Ethiopia Reburial;" Reggae.com
16. Hausman 171

Postlude: Very Fast Running

1. Rambali, 138–9; Ethiopians.com

Works Cited

"Abyssinia: Coronation." *Time* 3 November 1930: 23–24.

"Abyssinian Legends." *Times Literary Supplement* 1 June 1922: 360.

Acton, Roger. *The Abyssinian Expedition and the Life and Reign of King Theodore.* London: Illustrated London News, 1868.

Ashkenazi, Michael and Fran Markowitz. "Introduction: Sexuality and Prevarication in the Praxis of Anthropology." *Sex, Sexuality, and the Anthropologist.* Ed. Fran Markowitz and Michael Ashkenazi. Urbana and Chicago: University of Illinois Press, 1999.

Barrett, Leonard E., Sr. *The Rastafarians.* Boston: Beacon, 1997.

Bartleet, E.J. *In the Land of Sheba.* Birmingham: Cornish Brothers, 1934.

Bates, Darrell, Sir. *The Abyssinian Difficulty: the Emperor Theodorus and the Magdala Campaign, 1867–68.* Oxford: Oxford University Press, 1979.

Bay Area Author Mixes History and Romance in Newest Novel Release. 8 September 2006. Press release. Available: http://www.emediawire.com/releases/2006/09/prweb434859.htm.

BBC. *Marley's Fans Gather in Ethiopia.* 1 Feb. 2005. Available: http://news.bbc.co.uk/1/hi/world/africa/4225239.stm.

Beckingham, C.F., ed. *Travels to Discover the Source of the Nile by James Bruce.* New York: Horizon, 1964.

Bender, M.L., J.D. Bowen, R.L. Cooper, and C.A. Ferguson, ed. *Language in Ethiopia.* London: Oxford University Press, 1976.

Benedict, Ruth. *Patterns of Culture.* New York: Penguin, 1946.

Bolton, Melvin. *Ethiopian Wildlands.* London: Collins and Harvill, 1976.

Boot, Adrian and Chris Salewicz. *Bob Marley: Songs of Freedom.* Ed. Rita Marley. New York: Viking Studio Books, 1995.

Boswell, James. *Life of Johnson.* 1953. Ed. R.W. Chapman. New York: Oxford University Press, 1980.

Bovill, E.W. *The Niger Explored.* London: Oxford University Press, 1968.

Boyle, John, Fifth Early of Cork and Orrery. *Remarks on the Life and Writings of Dr. Jonathan Swift.* Ed. João Fróes. Newark: University of Delaware Press, 2000.

Bredin, Miles. *The Pale Abyssinian: A Life of James Bruce, African Explorer and Adventurer.* London: Harper Collins, 2000.

Briggs, Philip. *Guide to Ethiopia*. Old Saybrook, Conn.: Globe Pequot Press, 1995.

Brodie, Fawn M. *The Devil Drives: A Life of Sir Richard Burton*. New York: W.W. Norton, 1967.

Bruce, James. *Travels to Discover the Source of the Nile, in the Years 1768, 1769, 1770, 1771, 1772, and 1773*. 5 vols. Edinburgh: Printed by J. Ruthven, for G.G.J. and J. Robinson, Paternoster-Row, London, 1790.

Burke, Edmund. *A Philosophical Enquiry into the Origin of Our Ideas of the Sublime and Beautiful*. Ed. J.T. Boulton. Notre Dame, Ind.: University of Notre Dame Press, 1968.

Burton, Sir Richard. *First Footsteps in East Africa; or, an Exploration of Harar*. Ed. Isabel Burton. Memorial ed. 2 vols. London: Tylston and Edwards, 1894.

———. *Personal Narrative of a Pilgrimage to Al-Madinah and Meccah*. Memorial ed. 2 vols. London: Tylston and Edwards, 1894

Busk, Douglas. *The Fountain of the Sun: Unfinished Journeys in Ethiopia and the Ruwenzori*. London: Max Parrish, 1957.

Buxton, David. *Travels in Ethiopia*. London: Lindsay Drummond, 1949.

Caillou, Alan. *Sheba Slept Here*. New York: Abelard-Schuman, 1973.

Chard, Chloe. *Pleasure and Guilt on the Grand Tour: Travel Writing and Imaginative Geography, 1600–1830*. Manchester: Manchester University Press, 1999.

Cheesman, R.E. *Lake Tana & the Blue Nile: an Abyssinian Quest*. London: Macmillan, 1936.

Climbhotrock.com. *Lost Mountain*. Website. Available: http://www.climbhotrock.com/hotrockroot/stories/wehni/wehni2.htm.

Crockford's Clerical Directory for 1865: being a Biographical and Statistical Book of Reference for Facts relating to the Clergy and the Church. Third issue, 1865. Edinburgh: Peter Bell, 1995.

Cumming, Sir Duncan. *The Gentleman Savage: The Life of Mansfield Parkyns, 1823–1894*. London: Century, 1987.

Curling, Jonathan. *Edward Wortley Montagu, 1713–1776: The Man in the Iron Wig*. London: Andrew Melrose, 1954.

Davis, Stephen. "Introduction." *The First Rasta: Leonard Howell and the Rise of Rastafarianism*. Chicago: Lawrence Hill Books, 2003.

Digital Tradition Mirror—Rivers of Babylon. Available: http://sniff.numachi.com/pages/tiRIVBAB.html.

Dufton, Henry. *Narrative of a Journey through Abyssinia in 1862–3*. 2nd ed. 1867. n.p.: Elibron Classics, 2005.

Eliot, Simon. "Hotten, John Camden (1832–1873)." *Oxford Dictionary of National Biography.* Oxford: Oxford University Press, 2004.

Ethiopians.com. *Abebe Bikila (1932–1973).* Website. Available: http://www.ethiopians.com/abebe_bikila.htm.

Fanpage, Melodymakers.de: The Marley Family. *Thorough Major Remake on Meskel Square for Marley's Tribute.* Website. Available: http://www.melodymakers.de/forum/showthread.php?t=3237.

Ferguson, Lionel. *Into the Blue: The Lake Tana Expedition, 1953.* London: Collins, 1955.

Fleeman, J.D. *A Bibliography of the Works of Samuel Johnson: Treating His Published Works from the Beginnings to 1984.* Oxford: Clarendon Press, 2000.

Forbes, Duncan. *The Heart of Ethiopia.* London: Robert Hale & Co., 1972.

Frye, Northrop. *Anatomy of Criticism: Four Essays.* Princeton, N.J.: Princeton University Press, 1957.

Garvey, Marcus. *The Philosophy and Opinions of Marcus Garvey; or, Africa for the Africans.* 1923. The New Marcus Garvey Library. Dover, Mass.: The Majority Press, 1986.

Gold, Joel J. "Introduction." *A Voyage to Abyssinia.* The Yale Edition of the Works of Samuel Johnson, Vol. 15. New Haven, Conn.: Yale University Press, 1985.

Grundy, Isobel. *Lady Mary Wortley Montagu.* New York: Oxford University Press, 1999.

Halsband, Robert, ed. *The Complete Letters of Lady Mary Wortley Montagu.* Vol. 1. Oxford: Clarendon Press, 1965.

Hanson, Herbert M. and Della. *For God and Emperor.* Mountain View, Calif.: Pacific Press Publishing Association, 1958.

Hausman, Gerald, ed. *The Kebra Nagast: The Lost Bible of Rastafarian Wisdom and Faith from Ethiopia and Jamaica.* New York: St. Martin's Press, 1997.

Hayter, Frank E. *In Quest of Sheba's Mines.* London: S. Paul & Co., 1935.

———. *The Gold of Ethiopia.* London: S.Paul & Co., 1936.

Heffner, Edna S. *Ethiopia: Land Beyond the Rift.* n.p.: Heffner, 1957.

Henze, Paul B. *Ethiopian Journeys: Travels in Ethiopia 1969–72.* London: Ernest Benn, 1977.

Hoover, Nora K. "Victorian War Corrrespondents G.A. Henty and H.M. Stanley: The 'Abyssinian Campaign' 1867–1868." Diss. Florida State University, 2005.

Hotten, J.C. *Abyssinia and Its People; or, Life in the Land of Prester John.* London: John Camden Hotten, 1868.

Houghton, Walter E., ed. 5 vols. *The Wellesley Index to Victorian Periodicals,* 1824–1900. Vol. 2. Toronto and Buffalo: University of Toronto Press, 1966–1989.

The Imperial Archive: Key Concepts in Postcolonial Studies. 2007. School of English, Queen's University of Belfast. Available: http://www.qub.ac.uk/schools/SchoolofEnglish/imperial/key-concepts/Going-native.htm.

James, Henry. *Letters.* Ed. Leon Edel. 4 vols. Cambridge, Mass.: Belknap-Harvard University Press, 1984.

Johnson, Samuel. *The Idler and the Adventurer.* The Yale Edition of the Works of Samuel Johnson, Vol. 2. Ed. W.J. Bate, John M. Bullitt, and L.F. Powell. New Haven, Conn.: Yale University Press, 1963.

———. *A Journey to the Western Islands of Scotland.* The Yale Edition of the Works of Samuel Johnson, Vol. 9. Ed. Mary Lascelles. New Haven, Conn.: Yale University Press, 1971.

———. *The Rambler,* Vol. 1. The Yale Edition of the Works of Samuel Johnson, Vol. 3. Ed. W.J. Bate and Albrecht B. Strauss. New Haven, Conn.: Yale University Press, 1969.

———. *The Rambler,* Vol. 3. The Yale Edition of the Works of Samuel Johnson, Vol. 5. Ed. W.J. Bate and Albrecht B. Strauss. New Haven, Conn.: Yale University Press, 1969.

———. *Rasselas and Other Tales.* The Yale Edition of the Works of Samuel Johnson, Vol. 16. Ed. Gwin J. Kolb. New Haven, Conn.: Yale University Press, 1990.

———. *A Voyage to Abyssinia.* The Yale Edition of the Works of Samuel Johnson, Vol. 15. Ed. Joel J. Gold. New Haven, Conn.: Yale University Press, 1985.

Kapuściński, Ryszard. *The Emperor: Downfall of an Autocrat.* 1978. Trans. William R. Brand and Katarzyna Mroczkowska-Brand. New York: Vintage, 1983.

Kaufman, Michael T. "Ryszard Kapuściński, Polish Writer of Shimmering Allegories and News, Dies at 74." *New York Times* 24 January 2007: C14.

Kolb, Gwin J. "Introduction." *Rasselas and Other Tales.* The Yale Edition of the Works of Samuel Johnson, Vol. 16. New Haven, Conn.: Yale University Press, 1990.

———. "Textual Cruxes in *Rasselas.*" *Johnsonian Studies.* Ed. Magdi Wahba. Cairo, 1962.

Lawrence, T.E. *Seven Pillars of Wisdom: A Triumph.* Garden City, N.Y.: Doubleday, Doran, & Co., 1936.

Leask, Nigel. *Curiosity and the Aesthetics of Travel Writing, 1770–1840: "From an Antique Land."* Oxford: Oxford University Press, 2002.

Lee, Hélène. *The First Rasta: Leonard Howell and the Rise of Rastafarianism.* 1999. Trans. Lily Davis. Chicago: Lawrence Hill, 2003.

"A Letter from Edward Wortley Montagu, Esquire, F.R.S. To William Watson, M.D. F.R.S. Containing an Account of His Journey from Cairo, in Egypt, to the Written Mountains, in the Desart of Sinai." *Philosophical Transactions of the Royal Society* 56 (1766): 40–57.

Levine, Donald N. *Greater Ethiopia: The Evolution of a Multiethnic Society.* 1974. 2nd ed. Chicago: University of Chicago Press, 2000.

———. *Wax and Gold: Tradition and Innovation in Ethiopian Culture.* Chicago: University of Chicago Press, 1965.

The Literary World: Choice Readings from the Best New Books and Critical Reviews.

Lovell, Mary S. *A Rage to Live: A Biography of Richard and Isabel Burton.* New York: W.W. Norton, 1998.

Ludolf, Job. *A New History of Ethiopia. Being a Full and Accurate Description of the Kingdom of Abessinia, Vulgarly, Though Erroneously Called the Empire of Prester John.* In Four Books. London: Printed for Samuel Smith, 1682.

Lyons, Andrew P. and Harriet D. Lyons. *Irregular Connections: A History of Anthropology and Sexuality.* Lincoln: University of Nebraska, 2004.

Maitland, Alexander. *Wilfred Thesiger: The Life of the Great Explorer.* London: Harper Collins, 2006.

Marsden, Philip. *The Chains of Heaven: An Ethiopian Romance.* New York: Harper Collins, 2005.

Marsden-Smedley, Philip. *A Far Country: Travels in Ethiopia.* London: Century, 1990.

Mercury, Karen. *The Four Quarters of the World.* n.p.: Medallion Press, 2006.

Mitchell, Anthony. "Ethiopia Reburial for Bob Marley." *Guardian* 13 Jan. 2005.

Moore, W. Robert. "Coronation Days in Addis Ababa." *National Geographic* June 1931: 738–46.

Morell, Virginia. *Blue Nile: Ethiopia's River of Magic and Mystery.* Washington, D.C.: Adventure Press, 2001.

Morris, William. *The Earthly Paradise.* 1868–70. Ed. Florence S. Boos. 2 vols. New York: Routledge, 2002.

Munro-Hay, S.C. *Ethiopia, the Unknown Land: A Cultural and Historical Guide.* London: I.B. Tauris, 2002.

Murphy, Dervla. *In Ethiopia with a Mule.* 1968. London: Arrow, 1991.

Murrell, Nathaniel Smith, William David Spencer, and Adrian Anthony McFarlane, ed. *Chanting Down Babylon: The Rastafari Reader.* Philadelphia: Temple University Press, 1998.

Nesbitt, L.M. *Hell-Hole of Creation: The Exploration of Abyssinian Danakil.* New York: Knopf, 1935.

New Times and Ethiopia News 1936–56.

Nicolson, Marjorie Hope. *Mountain Gloom and Mountain Glory: The Development of the Aesthetics of the Sublime.* New York: W.W. Norton, 1959.

Once Upon a Romance: Interview with Karen Mercury. May 2005. Available: http://onceuponaromance.net/KarenMercuryInterview.html.

Pakenham, Thomas. *The Mountains of Rasselas: An Ethiopian Adventure.* New York: Reynal & Co., 1959.

———. *The Scramble for Africa, 1876–1912.* London: Weidenfeld and Nicolson, 1991.

Pankhurst, Richard. *The Ethiopians: A History.* Oxford: Blackwell, 1998.

———. "Mahbuba, the Beloved: The Story of a 19th-Century Ethiopian Slave-Girl." *Capital* 12 November 2006.

———. *Sylvia Pankhurst, Counsel for Ethiopia: A Biographical Essay on Ethiopian, Anti-Fascist and Anti-Colonialist History, 1934–1960.* Hollywood, Calif.: Tsehai, 2003.

Pankhurst, Sylvia. *Ethiopia: A Cultural History.* Essex: Lalibela House, 1955.

Parkyns, Mansfield. *Life in Abyssinia: Being the Notes Collected During Three Years' Residence and Travels in That Country.* 2 vols. New York: D. Appleton & Co., 1856.

Patey, Douglas Lane. *The Life of Evelyn Waugh.* Oxford: Blackwell, 1998.

Pindar, Peter. *The Works of Peter Pindar.* 4 vols. London: Walker and Edwards, 1816.

Pratt, Mary Louise. *Imperial Eyes: Travel Writing and Transculturation.* London: Routledge, 1992.

The Publishers' Weekly: the American Book Trade Journal.

Pye-Smith, Charlie. *The Other Nile.* New York: Viking, 1986.

The Queen of Sheba & Her Only Son Menyelek; Being the History of the Departure of God & His Ark of the Covenant from Jerusalem to Ethiopia, and the Establishment of the Religion of the Hebrews & the Solomonic Line of Kings in That Country. Trans. Edward A. Wallis Budge. London: Medici Society, 1922.

Rambali, Paul. *Barefoot Runner: The Life of Marathon Champion Abebe Bikila.* London: Serpent's Tail, 2006.

Reggae.com. *Let Bob Marley Rest in Peace.* 2004. Web site. Available: http://www.reggae.com/artists/bob_marley/restinpeace.htm.

Rey, Charles F. *Unconquered Abyssinia as It Is Today.* London: Seeley, Service & Co., 1923.

Romero, Patricia W. *E. Sylvia Pankhurst: Portrait of a Radical.* New Haven, Conn.: Yale University Press, 1987.

Rushby, Kevin. *Chasing the Mountain of Light: Across India on the Trail of the Koh-I-Noor Diamond.* London: Constable, 1999.

———. *Eating the Flowers of Paradise: A Journey through the Drug Fields of Ethiopia and Yemen.* New York: St. Martin's Press, 1999.

———. *Hunting Pirate Heaven: In Search of Lost Pirate Utopias.* New York: Constable, 2007.

———. *Paradise: A History of the Idea That Rules the World.* New York: Carroll and Graf, 2007.

Said, Edward. *Orientalism.* New York: Pantheon, 1978.

Shah, Tahir. *In Search of King Solomon's Mines.* New York: Arcade, 2002.

———. *Trail of Feathers: In Search of the Birdmen of Peru.* New York: Arcade, 2001.

Shakespeare, William. *Love's Labours Lost.* Oxford Shakespeare. Ed. Stanley Wells and Gary Taylor. Oxford: Oxford University Press, 2005.

Shaw, Len. *Into the Hidden Land.* London: John Gifford, 1970.

Shelemay, Kay Kaufman. *A Song of Longing: An Ethiopian Journey.* Urbana and Chicago: University of Illinois Press, 1991.

Silverberg, Robert. *The Realm of Prester John.* 1972. London: Phoenix Press, 2001.

Southard, Addison E. "Modern Ethiopia: Haile Selassie the First, Formerly Ras Tafari, Succeeds to the World's Oldest Continuously Sovereign Throne." *National Geographic* June 1931: 679–738.

Starkie, Enid. *Arthur Rimbaud.* New York: New Directions, 1961.

Steele, John. "King Solomon's Mines Found in Wilds of Abyssinia." *Chicago Tribune* 28 July 1935: D10.

Stewart, Julia. *Eccentric Graces: Ethiopia and Eritrea through the Eyes of a Traveler.* Lawrenceville, N.J.: Red Sea Press, 1999.

Summerskill, Mimi LaFollette. *In the Land of Solomon and Sheba.* Lawrenceville, N.J.: Red Sea Press, 2002.

Swift, Jonathan. *The Correspondence of Jonathan Swift.* Ed. Harold Williams. 5 vols. Oxford: Clarendon Press, 1963.

Thesiger, Wilfred. *The Danakil Diary: Journeys through Abyssinia, 1930–34.* London: Harper Collins, 1996.

———. *The Life of My Choice.* London: Collins, 1987.

Thirdfield.com. *Bob Marley Lyrics—"Chanting Down Babylon".* Available: http://www.thirdfield.com/html/lyrics/chantdown.html.

———. *Bob Marley Lyrics: "Is This Love."* Available: http://www.thirdfield.com/html/lyrics/isthislove.html.

The Times 9 October 1867: 11.

Tonkin, Thelma. *Ethiopia with Love.* London: Hodder and Stoughton, 1972.

Toy, Barbara. *In Search of Sheba: Across the Sahara to Ethiopia.* London: John Murray, 1961.

Ullendorff, Edward. *The Two Zions: Reminiscences of Jerusalem and Ethiopia.* New York: Oxford University Press, 1988.

Veitch, Sophie F. F. *Views in Central Abyssinia. With Portraits of the Natives of the Galla Tribes, taken in pen and ink under circumstances of peculiar difficulty, by T.E., a German traveller, believed at present to be one of the captives there. With descriptions by Sophie F. F. Veitch.* London: J.C. Hotten, 1868.

Waterfield, Gordon, ed. *First Footsteps in East Africa by Sir Richard Burton.* New York: Praeger, 1966.

Waugh, Evelyn. *Black Mischief.* New York: Farrar & Rinehart, 1932.

———. *The Diaries of Evelyn Waugh.* Ed. Michael Davie. London: Weidenfeld and Nicolson, 1976.

———. *The Essays, Articles and Reviews of Evelyn Waugh.* Ed. Donat Gallagher. London: Methuen, 1983.

———. *Remote People.* 1931. London: Methuen, 1991.

———. *Waugh in Abyssinia.* 1936. London: Methuen, 1984.

———. *When the Going Was Good.* Boston: Little, Brown, 1947.

Wheeler, Post. *The Golden Legend of Ethiopia: The Love-Story of Mâqedâ, Virgin Queen of Axum & Shêbâ, & Solomon the Great King.* New York: D. Appleton, 1936.

Woodhead, Leslie. *A Box Full of Spirits: Adventures of a Film-Maker in Africa.* London: Heinemann, 1987.

Wrong, Michela. *I Didn't Do It for You: How the World Betrayed a Small African Nation.* New York: Harper Perennial, 2005.

Zander, Eduard. *Das Skizzenbuch Eduard Zanders (1813–1868): Ansichten aus Nordäthiopien (1852–54).* Ed. Dorothea McEwan, Gerd Gräber, Johannes Hock. Köthen: Verein für Anhaltische Landeskunde, 2006.

Index

The authorized representative in the EU for product safety and compliance is:
Mare Nostrum Group
B.V Doelen 72
4831 GR Breda
The Netherlands

www.ingramcontent.com/pod-product-compliance
Lightning Source LLC
Chambersburg PA
CBHW030250100426
42812CB00002B/382